VERSE ABUSE

The unfortunate misuse of Biblical Passages

Dr. Allen V. Smith

Published by Papito Publishing Co.
P.B. Box 75535
Los Angeles, CA 90005
(323) 559-5840

Scripture quotations are from the Authorized New American Standard Bible and the King James Version Bible unless otherwise stated.

Acknowledgments

I thank God most of all for the inspiration and the courage to write this book, to my wife Lynette and our children for their patience and my family and friends for their support. I am grateful for all of the training I received from my early years by Apostle A.D. Noble, Dr. Charles Queen, Dr. Trimble, Dr. Hardin, and Dr. Robert Morey, whose leadership has been extremely appreciated. I am grateful for all of the opportunities and support given by the Ministerial Training Institute and Long Beach Bible Institute. I would also like to thank all of the Churches who've opened their arms of support allowing my ministry to flourish.

Introduction

Not only does the world face challenges with child abuse, drug abuse, alcohol abuse, elderly abuse and spousal abuse, but we are faced with the crisis of Verse Abuse. This is an abuse of the Bible. Too often we have heard, "The Bible said . . ." when the Bible never said that! This problem of taking biblical passages out of context is a bigger problem than we think! Our Nation is based on Judeo Christian ethics and values. If our interpretations of those values are wrong, then our standards will be wrong. It is important that we have a proper interpretation of what the Bible says since the very fabric of our policies are based upon it. Laws are based upon legislated morality. If our morality is convoluted, then our laws will be "twisted." When a society is basing its principles upon Scripture, but the interpretation of that Scripture isn't true, then we ultimately destroy the very thing that gives us our existence and that is the Word of God!

How do we know that the Bible is Gods Word?

The most obvious is that we have the inner witness of the Holy Spirit (Luke 24:32; John 16:13-14). Although this argument is used by other religious groups, this isn't the only and absolute acid test.

Every letter of the original manuscript is without error. There are apparent contradictions in the Bible, but mostly from copyist errors, or text being added by translators with poor knowledge of Hebrew and Koine Greek. But every word in the original autographs is true without error. We have copies of this original document. With all of our copies we can point to the original text and verify its accuracy. (For more information see Faith Defenders.com or the

Christian Research Institute.org.) Scientific facts support it. Archaeological evidence supports it.

The Need for Hermeneutics

Hermeneutics is defined as the art and the science of biblical interpretation. It is how we study the Bible and how we interpret what the Bible teaches and not what we think or feel the Bible should be saying. The process of Hermeneutics looks at the Bible as a collection of 66 different pieces of ancient Jewish manuscript and digs into it for the understanding of the text. The study of Hermeneutics helps us to observe the syntax and grammar, observe the literary units of each passage and chapter that that passage is in, and discerns what the author is saying about the Scripture. This higher Critical Theory cannot be applied to Homer, Plato, Aristotle, Shakespeare or contemporary works because the Bible is different from these writings. Not only is an academic approach necessary, but one has to be filled with the Spirit of God to get a more complete understanding of God's Word.

This book, Verse Abuse, helps us to get a correct understanding of some of the most common misapplied Scriptures in the Bible. There are hundreds of passages that are taken out of context, thus allowing false teaching to pollute Christianity. However, I have selected just a few to get us thinking, and hopefully put us on the right track.

CHAPTER 1

THE "GAP THEORY" IS NOT BIBLICAL

GENESIS CHAPTER 1

The "Gap Theory" argues that God had to re-create the universe that He initially created. The theory states that He had to destroy it because it was too wicked. It also argues that there was a pre-Adamic race (people that were created before Adam and Eve) that lived on the first earth and caused great evil. However this method of understanding is easily refuted by Scripture. The Gap Theorists claim that there is a break in the Hebrew Scripture. The Hebrew is specific

in how it translates this prepositional phrase. There is no break in the Hebrew which would allow such a theory to manifest. The Gap theory is simply a theory that exists because of a lack of biblical understanding.

א בְּרֵאשִׁית, בָּרָא אֱלֹהִים, אֵת הַשָּׁמַיִם, וְאֵת הָאָרֶץ.	1 In the beginning God created the heaven and the earth.
ב וְהָאָרֶץ, הָיְתָה תֹהוּ וָבֹהוּ, וְחֹשֶׁךְ, עַל-פְּנֵי תְהוֹם; וְרוּחַ אֱלֹהִים, מְרַחֶפֶת עַל-פְּנֵי הַמָּיִם.	2 Now the earth was unformed and void, and darkness was upon the face of the deep; and the spirit of God hovered over the face of the waters.

The periods did not exist in the original Hebrew. According to the King James Version, "In the beginning God created the heaven and the earth. And the earth was without form, and void; and darkness was upon the face of the deep." The original Hebrew text did not have verse divisions. According to many Hebrew scholars Moses wrote one sentence that we have artificially broken into two verses. The correct translation should read as follows: When the beginning began, God created out of nothing, the heavens and the earth, and the earth was (after its creation) formless and void, and darkness was over the surface of the deep, and the Spirit of God was hovering over the surface of the water.

The use of the w vav consecutive "and" as the first word in verse two usually means that the sentence is continuing. This is why many Hebrew scholars believe that the Hebrew sentence which began in verse one is not a separate sentence from verse two. The argument states that God created the heavens and the earth perfect and beautiful in their beginning and that at some subsequent period, how remote we cannot tell, the earth had passed into a state of utter desolation, and was void of all life. Not merely had its fruitful places become a wilderness, and all its cities been broken down; but the very light of its sun had been withdrawn; all the moisture of its atmosphere had sunk upon its surface; and the vast deep, to which God has set bounds that are never transgressed except when wrath has gone forth from Him, had burst those limits; so that the ruined planet, covered above its very mountain tops with the black floods of destruction, was rolling through space in a horror of great darkness.

Why would God allow something so catastrophic to happen to something so beautiful? Wherefore had God thus destroyed the work of His hands? If we may draw any inference from the history of our own race, sin must have been the cause of this hideous ruin: sin, too, which would seem to have been patiently borne through long ages, until at length its cry increased to Heaven, and brought down utter destruction. For, as the fossil remains clearly show, not only were disease and death inseparable companions of sin, then prevalent among the living creatures of the earth, but even ferocity and slaughter. And the fact proves that these remains have nothing to do with our world; since the Bible declares that all things made by God during the six days were very good, and that no evil was in them till Adam sinned.

Through his fall the ground was cursed, and it was doubtless at the same time that the whole creation was subjected to that vanity of fruitless toil, of never-ceasing unrest, and of perpetual decay, in which it has since groaned and travailed in pain together until now (Rom.8:22). When thorns and thistles sprang out of the earth, and its fertility was restrained, then that curse affected the animal kingdom also. There appeared in it a depraved and even savage nature which ultimately, though not perhaps in antediluvian times, reached its climax in a cruel thirst for blood, and completely changed the organization of some species. How this change was brought about, it is of course useless to speculate: for the hand of the Almighty wrought it.

God has allowed evil to manifest on this planet, but He is not the cause or the blame for the evil. He makes no mistakes. When the beginning began God started this creation process, and He will follow through with His plan until it is complete.

★

CHAPTER 2

THE EARTH WAS CREATED IN SIX LITERAL DAYS

GENESIS CHAPTER 1

Apparent Age

God created the Heaven and the Earth in six literal days. Some believe that it was created in 4.5 billion years. Others believe that it was created even over a longer period of time. The truth of the matter is that it was six literal days, with close to 24 hours in each day. It is true that many scientists have found certain archeological evidences, i.e. bones, ice glaciers, etc., which indicate an earth that is very old. However, the point that many of them miss is with what is known as "apparent age." When God created the heaven and the earth He created things that were already fully matured. For example, God had created a full grown, matured tree, but if you were to dissect that tree five minutes after God created it the tree could appear hundreds of years old. Remember Adam and Eve weren't created babies. They were of a young adult age.

The Rule of Yom

In the Hebrew language a rule exists which indicates that whenever you see the word "Yom" followed by a number it is taken in the sense of being literal not figurative. For example, if you have a "Yom" and it is connected to the "Echad' it indicates literal days. This rule cannot be refuted, because it is axiomatic throughout Scripture.

Top Soil Factor

Science has argued that the world is 4.5 billion years old. There are some who even say that it is older than that. However, there are questions that even the "great scientist" must answer. The top soil factor is among many of the facts that break down the theory of an "Old Earth Concept." It takes a thousand years to produce one inch of topsoil by the natural forces of erosion, such as wind and rain. If the world is 4.5 billion years old, the earth itself should have a thick layer of topsoil on its crust. Nevertheless, there is only an average of six to nine inches of this thousand year producing soil. The amount that we have can only explain thousands of years of erosion not millions. Where is the topsoil supporting billions of years of erosion?

The Ocean Floor Factor

One can then argue that the top soil created by billions of years of erosion has simply washed into the ocean and can be found in sedimentary deposits on its floor. If the earth is billions of years old and the erosion rate has been steady and of such a degree as to explain where all the topsoil went, the sediment at the bottom of the ocean should be miles deep. However, the sediment on the ocean floor only had .56 miles average of thickness. This depth can only explain thousands of years, and cannot represent billions of years of erosion. Where is the sediment created by billions of years of erosion?

The Meteor Factor

When meteors collide with the earth's atmosphere they disintegrate into dust that settles on the earth's surface. Given the present rate at which meteor dust is settling on the earth, if the earth is a billion years old there should be at least 54 feet of meteor dust on the surface of the planet. Since the depth of topsoil and ocean sediment do not contain billions of years of meteor dust, what happened to the dust?

The Helium Factor

As radioactive materials disintegrate, helium is released as a by-product into the atmosphere. Given the present rate at which helium is released into the atmosphere, if the earth is billions of years old, there should be enough helium in the atmosphere to make us all talk like Donald Duck. There is only enough helium in the atmosphere to explain thousands of years of disintegrated radioactive material. Where did the helium produced by millions of years go?

The Salty Sea Factor

Given the present rate at which salt and other minerals are being washed into the ocean, if the earth is billions of years old, what should be the concentration of salt in the earth's ocean? There is only enough salt in the ocean to explain thousands of years of erosion. The concentration of such minerals as nickel, as well as salt, in the earth's oceans would be many times greater if the earth were billions of years old. Where have all the billions of years of salt and other minerals gone?

The Earths Magnetic Field Factor

Current scientific evidence clearly indicates that the earth's magnetic field is decaying. With an understanding of the second law of thermodynamics by Sir Isaac Newton, the earth's magnetic field would have passed into nonexistence long ago. If the earth is billions of years old, why does it still have a magnetic field?

The Moon Dust Factor

The vehicles prepared for landing on the moon were equipped with special snowshoes because it was assumed that the moon is billions of years old, and there should be an incredibly thick layer of dust on the moon created by such things as meteor impact. They discovered only one-fourth of an inch of dust on the moon. This amount of dust can account for only thousands of years, not billions.

The Melting Sun Factor

The sun is shrinking as its energy is flung into the galaxy. Given the present rate of the shrinkage, if the earth is billions of years old, it should have disappeared by now. Or if the sun is billions of years old, in order for it to have shrunk down to the size it is now, it should have engulfed the space now occupied by most of the planets in this galaxy. If this is true, where did the planets come from?

The Volcano Factor

Since the earth's moon is a dead world with inactive volcanoes, it was assumed that this meant that the moon was billions of years old. It was also assumed that no moons would have active volcanoes. The evidence is now clear that at least one of the moons of Jupiter has active volcanoes. Does this fact not indicate that the assumption of the necessity of billions of years for the age of the universe is erroneous? As a matter of fact, if the universe is billions of years old, why and how should any planet or moon have active volcanoes?

The Saturn Rings Factor

If the universe is billions of years old we must assume that the rings of Saturn are of this age. Given the rate of orbital and structural decay, if the rings are billions of years old they should have collapsed into confusion. Yet, the evidence is clear that the rings are so distinct the rings must be viewed as young and not old. If the rings are billions of years old, why are they clear and distinct?

It is clear by the scientific evidences that the earth is much younger than it appears. Modern scientists have trouble trying to answer these questions. They much rather embrace a lie in order to avoid the fact that there must be a God who created all of this. However, let it be understood that this is a secondary issue, one that is to be debated, but not divided over.

Verse Abuse

★

CHAPTER 3

THERE WERE GIANTS ON THE EARTH

Genesis Chapter Six

Scripture clearly indicates that there is more evidence to believe that fallen angels had intercourse with women and produced giants on the earth, than the argument that a certain tribe of people invaded these women. Let us consider the material presented here which should make the point.

Background

Noah's faith triumphed over all corrupt reasoning. To rear so large a building, such a one as he never saw, and to provide food for the living creatures, would require from him a great deal of care, and labor, and expense. His neighbors would laugh at him. But through all such objections, Noah, by faith, got over; his obedience was ready and resolute. Having begun to build, he did not leave off till he had finished: so did he, and so must we do. He feared the deluge, and therefore prepared the ark. And in the warning given to Noah, there is a more solemn warning given to us, to flee from the wrath to come, which will sweep the world of unbelievers into the pit of destruction.

Christ, the true Noah, which same shall comfort us, hath by His sufferings already prepared the ark, and kindly invites us by faith to enter in. While the day of His patience continues, let us hear and obey His voice. He was a just man, justified before God, by faith in the promised Seed. As such He was made holy, and had right principles; and was righteous in His conversation. He was not only honest, but devout; it was His constant care to do the will of God. God looks down upon those with an eye of favor, who sincerely look up to Him with an eye of faith. It is easy to be religious when religion is in fashion; but it shows strong faith and resolution, to swim against the stream, and to appear for God when no one else appears for Him; Noah did so. All kinds of sin were found among men that fell from grace and went with Satan and are called the Nephilim.

The sons of God left their habitation in Heaven and found the women of Adam desirable. They proceeded to multiply their seed and bred with the women to produce Giants called the Gibur/Gibbor in the Hebrew. They corrupted God's worship as much as they could. The plot of Satan opened up in full scale and was like a sweeping army of locusts upon the earth devouring everything that stood in their way. Sin filled the earth with violence, and this fully justified God's resolution to destroy the world. The contagion of the offspring spread. When wickedness is become general, ruin is not far off; while there is a remnant of praying people in a nation, to empty the measure as it fills, judgments may be long kept off; but when all hands are at work to pull down the fences, by sin, and none stand in the gap to make up the breach, what can be expected but a flood of wrath? God told Noah His purpose to destroy the wicked world by water.

The secret of the Lord is with them that fear him, Psa.25:14. It is with all believers, enabling them to understand and apply the declarations and warnings of the written word. God chose to do it by a flood of waters, which should drown the world. As He chooses the rod with which He corrects His children, so He chooses the sword with which He cuts off His enemies. God established His covenant with Noah. This is the first place in the Bible where the word 'covenant' is found; it seems to mean: 1. The covenant of providence; that the course of nature shall be continued to the end of time. 2. The covenant of grace; that God would be a God to Noah and that out of his seed God would take unto Him a people. God directed Noah to make an ark. This ark was like the hulk of a ship, fitted to float upon the waters. It was very large, half the size of St. Paul's cathedral, and would hold more than eighteen of the largest ships now used. God could have secured Noah without putting him to any care, or pains, or trouble; but employed him in making that which was to be the means to preserve him, for the trial of his faith and obedience. Both the providence of God, and the grace of God, own and crown the obedient and diligent.

God gave Noah particular orders how to make the ark, which could not therefore but be well fitted for the purpose. God promised Noah that he and his family should be kept alive in the ark. What we do in obedience to God, we and our families are likely to have the benefit of. The piety of parents gets their children good in this life, and furthers them in the way to eternal life, if they improve it. So with Satan's plan in operation and sin prevailing, the spirit of the Lord which is Jesus Christ, the Holy Spirit, turned away from the violence and evil that can only come from the king of wickedness and his followers.

A study of Angelology would show that the Devil is a former glorified Angel. Because he is an Angel, he has the attributes and the characteristics of the others. By this we know that their powers are limited. He and his angels cannot be everywhere at the same time. He does not have all power. Yet he and his angels can materialize a body. Therefore, it is possible for an angel or a group of angels to have put on bodies and had intercourse with women, i.e. the "daughters of men."

Evidence #1

The first thing that we must establish is that according to the book of Job (the oldest book in the Bible) the phrase the "sons of God" made references to Angels and not a human race (Genesis 38:7, Psalm 29:1, Daniel 3:25). Therefore, it is not fair to the text to assume that it is referring to a tribe of people.

Evidence #2

The "sons of God" had sex with human females and produced giants called Nephilim. Moses wrote this without explanation, assuming that his audience already knew what he was talking about. The book of Job was the only book in existence before Moses wrote Genesis. The only possible literary reference would have been made from that book.

Evidence #3

The ancient Jews also believed this reference as it was indicated in the translation from the original Hebrew to the Alexandrine text of the Septuagint. This interpretation was also found in Josephus, the Apocryphal books, and the early Christian Church. Such early Christian writers as Justin, Clement, Alexander, Tertullian and Ambrose also carry this view. One writer argued saying that this could not be true because the Bible says in Matthew 22:30 that angels were not allowed to be married. Sad to say but I had to explain to him that you do not need to be married to have sex, although you're supposed to be. The angels were not thinking about marrying these women, they wanted them, and took them without reservation.

Evidence #4

In Genesis 19:5 the two good angels who visited Sodom were going to be raped by the homosexual mob if not protected by Lot. It is obvious that these angels had bodies that could be touched (Genesis 19:10).

Evidence #5

Genesis 6 is simply referring to mixed marriages between believers and unbelievers. Why did these mixed marriages produce giants? I am a product of mixed marriage and I'm only 6'tall.

Evidence #6

Why would God destroy the entire earth because some mixed marriages took place? Does it sound sensible to believe that God would destroy the entire world because some unbelievers married some believers? If God did it then why doesn't He do it now? How many people would be dead if He were to destroy all the mixed marriages?

In medieval European folklore, the incubus is a male demon (or evil spirit) who visits women in their sleep to lie with them in ghostly sexual intercourse. The woman who falls victim to an incubus will not awaken, although may experience it in a dream. Should she get pregnant the child will grow inside her as any normal child, except that it will possess supernatural capabilities. Usually the child grows into a person of evil intent or a powerful wizard. Legend has it that the magician Merlin was the result of the union of an incubus and a nun. A succubus is the female variety, and she concentrates herself on men. According to one legend, the incubus and the succubus were fallen angels.

Genesis 6:4 "There were giants in the earth in those days; and also after that, when the sons of God came in unto the daughters of men, and they bare children to them, the same became mighty men which were of old, men of renown." The words "giants," "sons of

God" and "mighty men" are all interconnected as the parent and offspring in scripture in the book of Genesis. "Giants" in the Hebrew is nephiyl; nephil nef-eel'; nef-eel' from the prime root word naphal naw-fal' A primitive root; to fall, in a great variety of applications (intransitively or causatively, literally or figuratively). "Sons of God" refers to angelic beings as described in the book of Job in Chapter 1 & 2. Job_1:6 and Job_2:1. "Mighty men" the Hebrew for this is gibbor gibbor ghib-bore', ghib-bore' Intensive from the same as; powerful; by implication warrior, tyrant. From the prime root word, gabar, is a primitive root; to be strong; by implication to prevail, act insolently. Hence, they were giants. Hence, fallen angels hence incubus (male) and female human offspring.

CHAPTER 4

ARABS ARE NOT CONNECTED TO THE ISRAELI PROMISE

Gen 37:25-28 Ishmaelites not Arabs

This is a touchy subject, because of the current pressure that is facing our world as it relates to Israel and the surrounding Arab countries. However, this issue needs to be addressed. I have heard time and time again this lie, that the Arabs have the promise to the land that was given to the Israelites. This may be a hard concept to embrace, but the Bible facts state the obvious and that is the land belongs to Israel.

The Middle East will never have peace until we answer the question, "Are the Arabs the Descendants of Ishmael?" The Arab's claim to the land of Israel rests entirely on three false assumptions:

1. All Arabs are the descendants of Abraham through Ishmael.
2. Ishmael and his descendants were included in the covenant God made with Abraham.
3. Since the Abarahamic covenant included the land of Israel, the Arabs have a legitimate claim to it.

According to the Torah, when Abraham left Ur of the Chaldees, he went west to what is now called Israel (Genesis 12). He became a dweller in tents in that land. It was in Israel that God made a covenant with him for the land in which he was living at the time. It was in Israel when he had Isaac, Ishmael, and many other sons and daughters. Isaac was the only son of Abraham chosen by God to be the heir of the covenant. Abraham took Isaac to Mt. Moriah to be offered up as a sacrifice to God.

The Torah is contradicted by Qur'an at nearly every point. According to the Koran, Surah 2:119-121, Abraham and Ishmael did not dwell in tents in Israel, but in the city of Mecca in Arabia. Together they rebuilt the Kabah and placed the black stone in the wall. It was Abraham who started the tradition of an annual pilgrimage to Mecca. Abraham took Ishmael (not Isaac) to nearby Mt. Moriah to be offered up as a sacrifice to God.

In Genesis 12:11-16, Ishmael's twelve sons were named Nebaioth, Kedar, Adbeel, Misbsam, Mishma, Dumah, Massa, Hadad, Tema, Jetur, Naphish, and Kedemah. These twelve sons intermarried with the local population in North Arabia and produced several nomadic tribes known as the Ishmaelites.

It was prophesied in the Torah that Ishmael and his family would "live to the east of all his brothers" (Genesis 16:12). "And they settled from Havilah to Shur which is east of Egypt as one goes toward Assyria" (Genesis 25:18). This broad area is the desert section east of Egypt in Northern Arabia toward the kingdom of the Assyrians.

The Ishmaelites are mentioned as a distinct tribe in Assyrian records. They later intermarried with and were absorbed by the Mideanites and other local tribes. In Genesis 37:25-28; 39:1, the Ishmaelites are called the Mideanites. In Judges 8:22-24, The Mideanites are called the Ishmaelites. The identification cannot be made any stronger. Arabia was already populated by the descendants of Cush and Shem long before Abraham or Ishmael were born (Genesis 10:7). Their cities and temples have been well documented by archaeologist. If all the Arab people descended from Ishmael as Muhammad claimed, where did all the original Arabs go? What happened to them? Who did Ishmael marry if the Arabs did not already exist? If Arabia was unpopulated, who built Mecca? Since he lived there, obviously it existed before, during, and after Ishmael started roaming the wilderness of North Arabia.

The descendants of Ishmael were scattered in Northern Arabia from the wilderness of Shur to the ancient city of Havilah. They were absorbed by the local tribes such as Mideanites (Genesis 37: 25-28). There is not historical or archaeological evidence that Ishmael went south to Mecca and became the "Father" of the Arab race. Some modern Arab scholars admit that before Muhammad, Qahtan was said to be the "Father" of the Arab people, not Ishmael. The Abrahamic covenant was given only to Isaac and to his descendants. Ishmael and the other sons of Abraham were explicitly excluded by God from having any part of the covenant made with Abraham (Genesis 18:18-21).

Therefore the descendants of Ishmael and the other sons of Abraham do not have any claim to the land of Israel, because they are not included in the covenant God made with Abraham. Only Jews have any claim to the land of Israel.

Summary of the False Assumptions

The first assumption has already been proven false. The Arab people are not all the descendants of Ishmael, and hence they are not the heirs of the patriarchs, the prophets, the Scriptures or the land of Israel. The claim that Muhammad went to Jerusalem is false. According to the Qur'an and the Hadith, Muhammad had a dream in the middle of the night in which he traveled through the sky, visited but was never actually in Jerusalem. The mosque on the temple site in Jerusalem is where Muhammad stood.

This may come as a shock to you but nowhere in the Qur'an does it state that Ishmael is the progenitor of the Arab race. Since it is not taught in the Qur'an, it cannot be a true Islamic belief.

CHAPTER 5

THE BIBLE DOESN'T SAY YOU CAN'T KILL

Exodus 20:13 thou shalt not shall not murder.

To kill is defined as:

1. To put to death
2. To deprive of life

To murder is defined as:

1. To kill (another human) unlawfully.
2. To kill brutally or inhumanly.

3. To put an end to; destroy: murdered their chances.
4. To spoil by ineptness; mutilate.

This Commandment should read thou shalt not murder, not kill. God Himself instructed His people to kill their enemy. Those of us who are familiar with the original Hebrew text of the Bible find frequent occasion to whine about inaccuracies and misleading expressions in the translations that are in use among non-Jews. Many of these discrepancies arose out of patently theological motives, as Christian interpreters rewrote passages in the "Old Testament" so as to turn them into predictions or prefigurations of the life of Jesus. Some of the mistranslations, though, are harder to account for.

For me, one of the most irksome cases has always been the rendering of the sixth commandment as "Thou shalt not kill." In this form, the quote has been conscripted into the service of diverse causes, including those of pacifism, animal rights, the opposition to capital punishment, and the anti-abortion movement.

Indeed, "kill" in English is an all-encompassing verb that covers the taking of life in all forms and for all classes of victims. That kind of generalization is expressed in Hebrew through the verb "harag." However, the verb that appears in the Torah's prohibition is a completely different one, "ratsah" which, it would seem, should be rendered "murder." This root refers only to criminal acts of killing.

It is, of course, not just a question of etymology. Those ideologies that adduce the commandment in support of their gentle-hearted causes are compelled to feign ignorance of all those other places in the Bible that condone or command warfare, the slaughter of sacrificial animals, and an assortment of methods for inflicting capital punishment. The Lord Himself after giving the commandment not to "kill" sent His people in battle to kill the enemy.

The good old King James version of the Bible, which introduced this formulation into standard English discourse, is usually much more accurate in its Hebrew scholarship, and I have wondered for many years how the erudite scholars who produced that fine translation managed to slip up on such a simple expression, one that would have been caught by any Jewish schoolchild. It turns out that the confusion did not originate with that sixteenth-century English translation. From the writings of Jewish exegetes who lived in medieval France, we learn that the gentiles in their environment were also translating the biblical prohibition incorrectly.

For example, two of the most eminent commentators of the time, Rabbi Samuel ben Meir (Rashbam) and Rabbi Joseph Bekhor-Shor, felt the need to go on at uncharacteristic length to explain that the Hebrew text refers only to unlawful killing. Both these scholars pointed out plainly the differences between the Hebrew roots for killing and murdering (for good measure. Bekhor Shor even provides a French translation of the latter term: meurtre), and brought ample evidence of the Torah's condoning other types of killing.

Rashbam concludes his discussion of the topic with the following words: And this is a refutation of the heretics, and they have conceded the point to me. Even though their own books state "I kill, and I make alive" (in Deuteronomy 32:39) --using the same Latin root as for "thou shalt not murder"--they are not being precise. From the words of these French Jewish scholars, we learn that the "thou shalt not kill" translation stems from the Latin Bible translation that was in use in the medieval Roman Catholic Church. Indeed, the Vulgate (as that translation is designated) employs the Latin verb occidere which has the sense of "kill" rather than "murder." By demonstrating that the Vulgate itself employed the root occidere in Deuteronomy, when the Almighty himself is speaking of his own power over the lives of his creatures--in a context where it cannot conceivably be rendered as "murder"--Rashbam aggressively proved the error of the traditional Christian understanding of the sixth commandment. It is not surprising, therefore, to hear that his Christian interlocutors acknowledged their error without a fight.

This still raises some difficult questions about the Latin Vulgate translation. The author of that translation, Saint Jerome (died in 420), spent much of his career in the Land of Israel, where he consulted frequently with Jewish scholars whose interpretations he often cites with great respect. Even the Septuagint, the old Greek translation of the Bible, translated the commandment with a word that means "murder" rather than "kill." St. Augustine, basing himself on the standard translations, made it clear that the commandment does not extend to wars or capital punishment that are explicitly ordained by God.

The fact remains, however, that even the Jewish translators were not unanimous in maintaining a consistent distinction between the various Hebrew roots. Don Isaac Abravanel and others noted that ratsah is employed in Numbers 35:27-30 both when dealing with an authorized case of blood vengeance, and with capital punishment--neither of which falls under the legal category of murder.

In fact, some distinguished Jewish philosophers believed that "thou shalt not kill" is a perfectly accurate rendering of the sixth commandment. Maimonides, for example, wrote that all cases of killing human beings involve violations of the command, even if the violation happens to be overridden by other mitigating factors. It has been suggested that this tradition underlies the virtual elimination of capital punishment in Rabbinic law. Viewed from this perspective, we may appreciate that the translation "thou shalt not kill" was not the result of simple ignorance on the side of Jerome or the King James English translators. Rather, it reflects their legitimate determination to reflect accurately the broader range of meanings of the Hebrew root.

As usual, careful study teaches us that what initially appeared ridiculously obvious is really much more complex than it seemed at first glance. We should be very cautious before passing hasty judgment on apparent bloopers. Thou shalt not kill doesn't mean you can't be a police officer or join the military. The Apostle Paul appealed for military protection from a death squad according to the book of Acts chapter 23:12-27. If Paul was a pacifist and viewed all armed military force as sinful, he would not have called them for help. Self defense has always been validated by Scripture ('if possible, as far as it depends on you, live at peace with everyone." Romans 12:18). Capital punishment was first implemented by God Himself.

In no way does the Scripture advocate violence unjustly, however, we have a responsibility to serve God and defend the faith which has been delivered unto the saints, in the book of Jude. If we ignore Scripture and attempt to appease the world, and in a sense love everyone to death, we too will die as a free nation and lose all of our civil liberties.

CHAPTER 6

THERE IS NO SUCH THING AS A GHOST

I Sam 28 no such thing as ghost

First Samuel 28:4-25 records a time when Saul was in a difficult situation and tried desperately to find out what he should do. God would not answer his prayers because he was in sin. So Saul went to a medium at Endor and asked her to call up his old friend Samuel from the "world beyond" so he could get some answers.

The medium held a séance for Saul. She was going through her ritual, when all of a sudden, something happened. The text indicates that this was not something she had planned. She got more than she had expected. This is important, the medium claimed that a form had appeared to her, and Saul assumed that the spirit of Samuel had indeed been brought back from the dead. But I don't believe it was Samuel. Many modern scholars agree it was actually a demon disguised as Samuel who appeared because:

Séances and medium ship are both condemned by God in Deuteronomy 18:9-11. In one of his better moments Saul had even made it illegal to engage in such activities (1 Samuel 28:9). If this practice was condemned by God, why would He allow it to take place? A medium referred to the manifestation as a "god" or "divine being" (verse 13). This can hardly refer to Samuel. Samuel was a man of great character. He would have him to humble himself and reject such praise. The very fact that "Samuel" allowed this to take place lends strength to the argument that it wasn't him at all. A medium does not have the power to call anyone back from the dead. Hebrews 9:27 reads, "And as it is appointed unto men once to die, but after this the judgment: So Christ was once the offered to bear the sins of many; and unto them that look for Him shall he appear the second time without sin unto salvation."

The medium was the only one who saw anything. Now look at the text very closely. Saul had to take her word for everything. Once you read the text you will see that the "witch" was the only one that supposedly saw Samuel. She described the "god" who appeared to her as being an old man wrapped in a robe (verse 14). If you really think about it this could have been anyone. She assumed that it was Samuel. Saul fell on his face and worshipped this being (verse 14). It is highly doubtful that Samuel would have allowed himself to be worshipped as a god. Samuel worshipped God. He would have never accepted the credit for being one.

Saul wanted Samuel to tell him that the future even though he admitted that God refused to tell him. But how could Samuel tell him about the future if God had already said no? Samuel could not know the future independently of God. This "Samuel" predicted that Saul and his sons would be killed by the Philistines the very next day. But this did not happen the next day.

Samuel could not have stated that Saul would be killed by the Philistines because Samuel killed himself in an act of suicide (1 Samuel 31:4, 5). This prophecy therefore, would be considered a false prophecy. The Bible gives us the acid test in identifying a false prophet in Deuteronomy 18. The way to know if a prophet is true is whether the prophecy comes to pass. Since this prophecy did not come to pass, Samuel would have to have been a false prophet.

Finally, people do not become ghosts when they die. There is no such thing a "Casper the friendly ghost." Any "ghost" that you see are demons, and or angels. The Bible gives no argument for a disembodied spirit. The Holy Ghost, and Jesus giving up the ghost, i.e. spirit, is but a few references.

As a result of this data, one must believe that this recall of Samuel was not actually Samuel. Some may disagree, like Hank Hanegraaff, of the Bible Answer Man broadcast, but with little to no counter position. He states that God just allowed it. Would God allow a man to be worshipped, supporting false prophecies, believing the testimony of a witch, etc? Do not think of this on an emotional level. Simply analyze the facts and you will be convinced that what you thought you believed could very well be different than what the Bible supports.

CHAPTER 7

SO, NOW WHAT DO WE DO...?

THERE ARE PHYSICAL BODIES IN HEAVEN

2 Kings 2:11 "And Elijah went up by a whirlwind to heaven." (NASB).

First off we must understand that the Bible presents to us three different heavens:

The first heaven is the air where the birds fly (Matthew 6:26).
The second heaven is where space and the stars are (Acts 7:42).

The third heaven is where Paradise where God rules (Matthew 6:9 and 10).

Now the third heaven is important because it is a place where physical bodies are as well as spiritual creatures and human souls. Christ's resurrection body is now in heaven: John 2:19-22; Hebrews 1:3. Enoch, according to Genesis chapter five is there as well as Elijah according to 2 Kings 2:11. The Bible also indicates various creatures are there such as angels (Hebrews 12:22), cherubim (Ezekiel chapter 10) and seraphim (Isaiah chapter 6). The souls/spirits of the believers are there as well (Hebrews 12:23; Revelation 6:9).

What will be waiting for us in heaven?

Allow me to spark your curiosity. While I cannot go into a lengthy discussion on this subject I will provide brief highlights to encourage you.

IN HEAVEN:

1. We will see loved ones who died in Christ (Genesis 25:8, 17; 35:29; Numbers chapter 31, Deuteronomy 32:50).

2. We will have divine comfort (Luke Chapter 16).

3. We will come into the treasures we sent up while on the earth (Matthew chapter 6, Luke chapter 12, I Timothy 6:17-19).

4. We will reach perfection (Hebrews 12:23).

5. A new name only for you (Revelations 3:12).

6. Gain (Philippians 1:21).

We will inherit the new earth and will fulfill the cultural mandate originally given to Adam (Revelations chapter 21, Matthew 5:5, Genesis 1:28).

The Bible declares that all those who have accepted Jesus Christ as their Savior will receive a new body fit for heaven and eternal life. Our present, earthly bodies are perishable and subject to death, but by God's power, in an instant, they shall be changed into a new body at the resurrection.

God's promise of eternal life is God's gift of salvation to all those who believe in Christ. I Corinthians 15:42 describes our resurrection of the dead. It is sown in corruption; it is raised in incorruption. I Corinthians 15: 50-57, Now this I say, brethren, that flesh and blood cannot inherit the kingdom of God; neither doth corruption inherit incorruption. Behold, I tell you a mystery: We all shall not sleep (die), but we shall all be changed, in a moment, in the twinkling of an eye, at the last trump: for the trumpet shall sound, and the dead shall be raised incorruptible, and we shall be changed.

For this corruptible must put on incorruption, and this mortal must put on immortality. But when this corruptible shall have put on incorruption, and this mortal shall have put on immortality, then it shall come to pass the saying that is written, Death is swallowed up in victory. O death, where is thy victory? O death, where is thy sting? The sting of death is sin; and the power of sin is the law: but thanks be to God, who giveth us the victory through our Lord Jesus Christ. This is also known as the rapture. It is written to the church and there will be believers living at the time this resurrection occurs. For those who claim that the rapture is a fallacy, the Apostle Paul says, "Now if Christ be preached that he rose from the dead, how say some among you that there is no resurrection of the dead? But if there be no resurrection of the dead, then is Christ not risen: And if Christ be not risen, then is our preaching vain, and your faith is also vain. Yea and we are found false witnesses of God; because we have testified of God that he raised up Christ: whom he raised not up, if so be that the dead rise not."

Evidence of the Afterlife, Luke 16:19-31.

19There was a certain rich man, which was clothed in purple and fine linen, and fared sumptuously every day:

20And there was a certain beggar named Lazarus, which was laid at his gate, full of sores,

21And desiring to be fed with the crumbs which fell from the rich man's table: moreover the dogs came and licked his sores.

22And it came to pass, that the beggar died, and was carried by the angels into Abraham's bosom: the rich man also died, and was buried;

23And in hell he lift up his eyes, being in torments, and seeth Abraham afar off, and Lazarus in his bosom.

24And he cried and said, Father Abraham, have mercy on me, and send Lazarus, that he may dip the tip of his finger in water, and cool my tongue; for I am tormented in this flame.

25But Abraham said, Son, remember that thou in thy lifetime receive thy good things, and likewise Lazarus evil things: but now he is comforted, and thou art tormented.

26And beside all this, between us and you there is a great gulf fixed: so that they which would pass from hence to you cannot; neither can they pass to us that would come from thence.

27Then he said, I pray thee therefore, father, that thou would send him to my father's house:

28For I have five brethren; that he may testify unto them, lest they also come into this place of torment.

29Abraham saith unto him, they have Moses and the prophets; let them hear them.

30And he said, Nay, father Abraham: but if one went unto them from the dead, they will repent.

31And he said unto him, If they hear not Moses and the prophets, neither will they be persuaded, though one rose from the dead.

- This passage of Scripture should be understood as a rabbinic parable. This is different from other parables because:
- The beggar must have been a real historical character because his name was given
- Abraham was a real historical character
- Parables don't ascribe personal names only titles and general terms.
-

In this rabbinic teaching we see that there is a conscious afterlife and not simple us disappearing from existence. One of the important factors to note is that we celebrate life; because once we are born we will live forever. We will receive everlasting punishment or everlasting bliss, but we will exist for ever and ever.

CHAPTER 8

THE APPLE OF MY EYE IS NOT A REAL APPLE

Psalm 17:8, not an apple, but daddy's little girl.

Apple of my eye

Often daughters or sons are referred to as the "apple" of their parent's eye. This phrase originates from King David, who wrote in Psalm 17 to ask God to remember and love David as His child: "Keep me as the apple of your eye, hide me in the shadow of your wings." (Ps 17:8).

No part of the body more precious, more tender: Verse 8. "Keep me as the apple of your eye." What is more carefully guarded than the eye; and of the eye, no portion more peculiarly to be protected than the central apple, the pupil, or as the Hebrew calls it, "the daughter of the eye." The all-wise Creator has placed the eye in a well-protected position; it stands surrounded by projecting bones like Jerusalem encircled by mountains.

Moreover, its great Author has surrounded it with many tunics of inward covering, besides the hedge of the eyebrows, the curtain of the eyelids, and the fence of the eyelashes; and, in addition to this, He has given to every man so high a value for his eyes, and so quick an apprehension of danger, that no member of the body is more faithfully cared for than the organ of sight. Thus, Lord, keep thou me, for I trust I am one with Jesus, and so a member of His mystical body. "Hide me under the shadow of Thy wings." Even as the parent bird completely shields her brood from evil, and meanwhile cherishes them with the warmth of her own heart, by covering them with her wings, so do Thou with me, most condescending God, for I am Thine offspring, and Thou hast a parent's love in perfection. This last clause is in the Hebrew in the future tense, as if to show that what the writer had asked for but a moment before he was now sure would be granted to him. Confident expectations should keep pace with earnest supplication.

A study in Hermeneutics and Hebrew, courses of which I currently teach, will help you understand the significance of Languages and proper biblical interpretation. Just because we read a biblical word in the English doesn't mean that that word has the same meaning in Scripture. Part of the reason many of us are confused is because we have been learning from verses which have been abused.

CHAPTER 9

CHRISTIANS ARE NOT SUPPOSED TO BE PACIFISTS

Matt. 5:9. . .blessed are the Peacemakers.

How do Pacifists try to establish their position in Scripture?

They avoid all passages which speak directly to the issue of the state using force to punish criminals and an army to protect the nation, particularly avoidance of Romans chapter 13. They often appeal to passages which in their contexts deal with the church or with the individual. Somehow modern theologians and lay people try to establish that the New Testament Church as a Church that should not use physical force in its discipline. Sow that on a day-to-day basis we should "go the second mile" and "turn the other cheek."

They make a jump from individual ethics to national ethics; apply to the State what was only applied to the Church or individual in Scripture; take general ethical statements which in their contexts apply to non-life-threatening situations (peacetime/not a wars situation) and apply them to national times of war or times when your life or the lives of others are threatened (examples: Romans chapter 12:17-21).

Why do they keep to vague generalities or statements not related to the Bible? They do not pay any attention to exegesis or to the Greek or Hebrew. They merely quote the text and give it a pacifist slant. Is the Bible a "Book of War" or a "Book of Peace"? Does it give a romantic view of man's nature and history, or is it filled with realistic descriptions of human depravity and violence? In other words, does the Bible manifest that its authors were pacifists, or does it manifest an attitude toward war and peace reflecting the "just war" position?

What kind of information regarding this subject would we find in the Bible? If the biblical authors were pacifists, we would expect to find more references to peace that war. Warfare would never be honored or glorified. Warriors would never be praised of lifted up as heroes. There would be clear condemnations of all wars, including wars involving God's people. God would not be pictured in a warlike manner. His people would never use force against evil. Peace would be exalted above war. Treaties would be more frequent than war. Slavery under tyranny would be viewed as more moral and desirable than war or revolution. God would never command or allow war in any situation whatsoever.

The Bible was written by the hands of men who viewed the use of force to overcome evil as a just cause for war or revolution. War and its warriors are glorified and exalted as righteous and holy before God. God Himself commanded His people to go to war. He is pictured as a God of War. His armies in Heaven and on earth are using force against evil and Satan's kingdom.

War is referred to 256 times, while peace in the sense of an absence of war is referenced only 28 times. Treaties are mentioned 18 times. Most of them were condemned by God because they were appeasements of aggressors. Israel learned by hard experience that all their treaties with Assyria, Babylon and Egypt ended in war. While peace treaties do work at times (Genesis 26:29) God generally took a dim view of treaties to appease tyrants (Deuteronomy 23:6).

Let's examine God's view on war

- God at times commanded His people to go to war in order to achieve peace; i.e., the purpose of such wars was peace! (Leviticus 26:3-8).

- Christ Himself is pictured as a warrior (Revelations 6:1-8; 1 Thessalonians 5:3).

- "Peace" can be used as a weapon to destroy a nation (Daniel 8:25). "By peace (He) shall destroy many."

- Permanent and universal peace will only be realized on earth when Jesus returns, the wicked are removed and the righteous perfected (Isaiah 65:17, 25).

- Wars, i.e. the use of force to over come evil, will be a part of human history until Jesus returns (Matthew 24:6-8).

- All Utopian hopes of peace on earth are doomed to failure as long as man is sinful by nature.

The word for peacemaker which was worn by Caesar was used to illustrate the enforcement of peace, in the event that things were to get out of control. I remember when my grandmother would tell us "you all better calm down in there before I come in and bust you up." She was enforcing peace. She was the peace maker, because she made it peaceful. This is the term that is described in Scripture. God wants us to be peaceful, but not passive. We are an active, vibrant people, and we need not be afraid of the enemy.

The Feminization of the Church

During the 19th Century we have learned of an attack on manhood. We have seen a rise of the feminization of Christianity. Jesus, for example, has been depicted as a weak, effeminate, white European male with a pale complexion and long hair set in a womanly manner. Most of these portraits were made by Michelangelo, who was not even a Christian, but an Atheist. We adopted his paintings a perception of Jesus and have embraced it as if it were biblically valid.

These were his ideas of how Christ looked. Since the time of the Renaissance he fooled the Catholic Church into accepting this lie. None of the portraits by Michelangelo and the other contemporary artist depict Jesus, a man who survived in the wilderness for forty days without food. What happened to the biblical Jesus who was strong and virile? What happened to the Jesus of the Bible who commanded the respect and allegiance of other men? This same Jesus who was strong enough to handle the hard work of carpentry and tough enough to flip tables and run out money changers? Now we sing songs like "sweet Jesus" and romantic songs with Him. We have made Him a long-haired, blond, blue-eyed California surfer! I thought He was "mighty God" Isaiah 9:6.

Today we have movies like *Fight Club*. This movie goes the other way. It showed young, non fathered men, who rebelled against their mothers and became hyper masculine. They wore the bruises as a badge of honor in a sick macho violent way attempting to identify with real manhood. Boys can no longer be boyish. We are attacking them for playing rough. Instead, we want to encourage our boys toward self-expression like the girls.

A real man is a man of peace. A real man is able to love and one who is able to be patient. He is a man who can cry and yet still be a man. Like the character played by Cuba Gooding in the movie Jerry Maguire. He was a man; although he cried, you would never deny his manhood. Hyper masculinity is not the answer to manhood. It is not a cure all for pacifism. It goes against the grain of what a real man is. A real man is a man who is chivalrous. I know that we forgot this word, but it is a man who in the days of King Arthur is the perfect knight embodied with piety, valor, gentleness, and compassion. A real man is a gentleman. A real man is educated and hard working. He is one who loves his family. Not the kind of man who will tape over his home movies with his son, just to make room for new footage with his young girlfriend, but a man who will stand up for what is right, even when the world thinks it's wrong.

We have boys today (like Homer's odyssey where Telemachus is in search of his missing father) who don't know who their father is. These are the boys that are in gangs, who are hyper masculine in search of a way to identify with manhood. Thank God for the mothers who have stepped up to the plate. It is said that in certain communities, particularly the black community, 70% of the children being raised are by single mothers. Where are the fathers? It is the responsibility of the man who chooses to lie down with a woman to raise the child. It is not the child's fault. It is time for men to raise boys into becoming men. A woman cannot raise a man like a man can. And, likewise, a man cannot teach a girl to be a woman. It was the design of God for both sexes to have a role in child development.

Conclusion

Being peaceful doesn't make us weak, but being a pacifist is against the very fabric of God's description of us in Scripture. We are to be strong and take responsibility for our actions. It is a hard, but necessary thing for us to do. I pray that God will give us the will and the courage to do the right thing.

CHAPTER 10

CHRISTIANS CAN MAKE RIGHTEOUS JUDGMENTS

Matthew chapter 7: hypocritical judgment.

One day I was looking at a television show where the panel was promoting immoral activity as if it were morally acceptable. A member of the audience stood up and said, "I am a Christian and this activity is sinful." The panelist immediately said "the bible says that you are not supposed to judge." The Christian man in the audience sat down quietly without saying another word. It was as if the only Scripture that the non Christian panelist knew was Matthew Chapter seven, "Judge not."

We should make judgments which are based on the yardstick of righteousness as revealed in his Word, which look beyond mere appearance, and which are also made with the right spirit in heart. When Jesus said "Judge not, that you be not judged" (Matt.7:1), He immediately shows what kind of judgment He is speaking of there. He obviously cannot mean that we must never make any kind of judgment at all; otherwise, we would not be able to fulfill the exhortations of the Word in numerous places, such as being told never to let anyone deceive us (please read Matt.24:4; Luke 21:8; 2 Thess.2:3; Eph.5:6; Colossians 2:8). If only God can judge, as you say, then how will we be able to fulfill the Apostle John's command: "Beloved, do not believe every spirit, but test the spirits, whether they are of God; because many false prophets have gone out into the world" (1 John 4:1)? Far from being wrong, judgment is actually a vital part of the Christian armory.

Christ has put pastors and teachers into the church precisely to make judgments which will prevent people from being "tossed to and fro and carried about with every wind of doctrine, by the trickery of men, in the cunning craftiness of deceitful plotting" (Eph.4:14). The judgment which the Lord Jesus forbids in Matt.7:1 (as the context very plainly shows) refers to a person who makes a judgment about another person when he himself is a practitioner of the very thing which he is judging in the other! That is hypocritical judgment, which is forbidden by Christ. But the kind of judgment which builds up God's people by advising them of danger and outright falsehood is an absolute necessity.

"Judge not, that ye be not judged. For with what judgment ye judge, ye shall be judged: and with what measure ye mete, it shall be measured to you again. And why beholdest thou the mote that is in thy brother's eye, but considerest not the beam that is in thine own eye? Or how wilt thou say to thy brother, Let me pull out the mote out of thine eye; and, behold, a beam is in thine own eye? Thou hypocrite, first cast out the beam out of thine own eye; and then shalt thou see clearly to cast out the mote out of thy brother's eye." - Matthew 7:1-5

You see – the verse actually ends up instructing us to "cast the beam out of our own eye" FIRST, BEFORE "pulling the mote out of our brother's eye" – NOT "Don't ever pull the mote out of your brother's eye". What Jesus was saying here is that others will judge us by the same standard we judge them so, DON'T BE A HYPOCRITE! Of course, the Christian life is not about pointing fingers at each other, but neither is it an all-access pass to free-for-all living in Jesus' name.

Another verse of scripture often used inaccurately to support the fictitious commandment: "Thou shalt not judge." is John 8:7b, where Jesus, addressing religious leaders concerning the woman caught in adultery, said:

"...He that is without sin among you, let him first cast a stone..." Again, liberals and well-meaning Christians alike stop and read no further than the word "stone", leaving the false impression that adultery really isn't such big deal after all and maybe sin in general isn't as bad as we once thought. Was Jesus telling them to keep their silence concerning adultery and be more tolerant of sin? NO! He was again teaching them to not be hypocrites – sending the woman away with specific instructions to "sin no more". (i.e., Stop your adulterous ways and repent) A very judgmental remark by today's standards, don't you think?

If there is to be no judging among Christians, how could we even have a legislative or judicial branch of government in this country? How could we be a responsible parent, a good teacher, a fair employer, a helpful counselor, an effective policeman, a powerful preacher, an accurate journalist or even a faithful friend? If judging others is as unchristian as today's liberal claims it is, how do you explain the often harsh and intolerant language of God's most faithful from the New Testament?

(John the Baptist to King Herod): "It is not lawful for thee to have thy brother's wife." - Mark 6:18

(The Apostle Paul): "When Peter came to Antioch, I opposed him to his face, because he was clearly in the wrong." - Galatians 2:11

(Stephen, speaking to the religious leaders before they stoned him to death):

"Ye stiff-necked and uncircumcised in heart and ears, ye do always resist the Holy Ghost: as your fathers did, so do ye. Which of the prophets have not your fathers persecuted? And they have slain them which showed before of the coming of the Just One; of whom ye have been now the betrayers and murderers: Who have received the law by the disposition of angels, and have not kept it." – Acts 7:51-53

(Jesus addressing the religious leaders):

"Woe unto you, scribes and Pharisees, hypocrites! for ye are like unto white sepulchers, which indeed appear beautiful outward, but are within full of dead men's bones, and of all uncleanness." - Matthew 23:27

"Ye serpents, ye generation of vipers, how can ye escape the damnation of hell?" - Matthew 23:33

"O generation of vipers, who hath warned you to flee from the wrath to come?" - Matthew 3:7b

"O generation of vipers, how can ye, being evil, speak good things? For out of the abundance of the heart the mouth speaketh." - Matthew 12:34

What about Jesus taking a whip to all of the moneychangers in the temple there in Matthew 21:12 and Mark 11:15? That's about as judgmental as it gets short of execution. If this doesn't sound like the

Jesus you know, it may be that you've been worshipping and serving the wrong God. For those of you who are still unconvinced – read here what the Apostle Paul had to say about Christians judging others:

"Do ye not know that the saints shall judge the world? And if the world shall be judged by you, are ye unworthy to judge the smallest matters? Know ye not that we shall judge angels? How much more things that pertain to this life" - 1st Corinthians 6:2-3

If all we do is tell the sinner "Jesus loves you" there's a good chance they'll mistakenly think they're saved. Only after they know they're lost and in danger of eternal damnation will they come to appreciate those three little words that mean so much and cry out to Him in repentance and faith.

We can judge someone on the basis of how he lives (John 7:24; Matthew 7:6, Galatians 5:19-21).

We can judge a culture on the basis of its laws, which are simply codified beliefs, values, and morals (Jeremiah 6:22-23; Titus 1:12-13).

We are told to judge but from a Scriptural basis. Our judgment is based on Divine intervention to weed out the intention of others. We need to have the Spirit of God lead us and direct us when we are encountering others. Our judgments should be based on love. For example, I believe that Sister Watermelon is in some financial trouble. Our judgment causes us to help her, by providing financial aid. Our judgments will determine whether or not a brother or sister is in need of counseling. We Judge righteously and not hypocritically. We have to consider our selves, because we are not perfect. We will sin and we will need the mercy of God in this life.

CHAPTER 11

A MODEL OF PRAYER

Luke Chapter 11, a model of how the disciples should pray.

This is only a model of which the Lord uses to teach His disciples how to pray. This was not meant to be the prayer that Jesus Himself uses. Within this model prayer we find a more effective way to come to learn more of the Lord. Let us examine the introduction of this prayer to establish the point.

"And it came about that while He was praying in a certain place, after He had finished, on of His disciples said to Him, "Lord, teach us to pray just as John also taught his disciples."

First, the disciples called Jesus "Lord" to acknowledge His Lordship over all of life including prayer. This means that you must submit to what the Bible teaches on prayer. You must not "lean to your own understanding" (Proverbs 3:5and 6).

Second, notice that John the Baptist taught his disciples to pray. We are not told how or in what way he taught them. But that he did so is clear from the disciple's request. If he had to teach his disciples that art and skill of effectual prayer, how can modern pastors excuse their failure to teach their people about prayer?

Third, the disciple asked Jesus to teach "us" to pray. Notice that He put it in the plural, "us" instead of the singular "me." Why? He wanted Jesus to instruct all the disciples in the art ad skill of prayer because they all needed instruction on this subject. No one is so smart that he does not need Special Revelation on prayer.

Fourth the word translated, "to pray" is proseucomenon. It is a present middle infinitive. The grammar of this verb indicates several things:

1) The present tense indicates that the disciples wanted instruction in prayer right there and then. He had just witnessed Jesus praying and this motivated him to ask Jesus how to pray.
2) The infinitive indicates that he was not asking for just one lesson on prayer. He wanted Jesus to make prayer a regular part of His discipleship program.
3) The middle voice indicates that he wanted Jesus Himself to do it, not just some other disciple. "Lord, you yourself teach us to pray."

The tragedy is that there are very few if any seminaries or Bible colleges that have courses on the theology of prayer. Since a prayerless ministry is a powerless ministry, could the lack of teaching on prayer be one of the reasons the Church is so weak today? There are insights on prayer that you cannot get from books or lectures. Only Christ Himself can personally teach us these things while we spend time in prayer with Him. Thus, prayer is experiential as well as academic. Ask the Lord to teach you about prayer.

Most prayer should consist of these basic principles. We know that our prayer is delivered by the Holy Ghost, processed by Jesus, to be received of the Father, yet He gives us insights on how we should address Him in prayer. One argument is that if the Holy Spirit takes our prayer, changes it, to be pure by the time it is received of the Father. So then why should we even bother with praying? Prayer does more for us then it does for God. It is an instrument that draws us closer to His will. We can become emboldened when we pray.

Our Prayer time should include reading the Scripture

Our prayer should include time of reading the Scripture, because the Scripture serves as a basis for our arguments. If we examine the Psalms, we will find legal arguments which we can present before the Lord when we pray. These arguments allow God to prove Himself while encouraging our faith. For Example:

Psalm 4:1, "Answer me when I call, O God of my righteousness! You have relieved me in my distress; Be gracious to me and hear my prayer."

In this passage the psalmist is saying, Lord answers me, because when I was down and out you answered me before. The argument is that you did it for me before, so on that basis please do it for me again. Another type of argument is based on the Scripture. When we go before God it is as if we are going to court. Jesus, our Advocate, is our lawyer. God the Father is the Judge and the Holy Spirit is the Jury. For example, when we go to court, in prayer, we are pleading for God to answer us based on something that was stated in Scripture. We can argue from His word. "You, master, said that your joy is our strength, and let the weak say that I am strong. So if I feel weak and have no strength, it is just temporary, because your word says that I can overcome this situation." If I feel weak right now, help me based on what you put in your word.

God cannot deny His word. This is why prayer is so important with our bibles, because it helps us to form legal, moral, spiritual arguments as to why God should do something for us.

A simple formula for prayer should include the following:

- Invocation. (This is the process by which we invite the Lord in to our hearts).
- Confession. (This is when we confess our sins).
- Worship. (When God is in our presence we can't help but to worship Him).
- Petition. (At this point we can ask what we want of Him).
- Intercession. (We than began to pray for others).
- Thanksgiving. (We thank God for hearing us and answering our prayer).

This is not the only formula, but it is an effective one. This pattern is seen throughout the Psalms, Book of Job, Ephesians, etc., as a model by which we can use to really make a connection with God through prayer. As we develop this pattern of prayer, we will find our prayer sessions lasting for hours. As a result of this pattern of prayer, we will began to see greater results in our lives.

CHAPTER 12

BORN FROM ABOVE, NOT BORN AGAIN

St. John 3:7 "… except a man be born again?"

Today the phrase "Born-again" not only has become entrenched stock Christian cliché but also the phrase into secular jargon so that it is commonly heard in advertising, sportscasting and movie dialogues. Where in God's Word does this phrase come from? Does the phrase appear at all in the God-breathed Text? Nor has it appeared in any Greek text?

The source typically quoted is Jesus speaking to Nicodemus in John 3:3, 7. There the KJV and NKJV read: "...unless one is born again he cannot see the Kingdom of God..." In verse 7 Jesus is quoted as saying: "Do not marvel that I said to you: 'You must be born again...'" But what does the God-breathed Greek Text say? John 3:3 says literally: "...except he might-be-begotten from-above, he is-not-able (same word means is-without-power) to experience the Reign of the God..." There is no mere notion of again here. The Greek God-Logic in both God-breathed and corrupt Greek manuscripts say simply: one must first be begotten from-above to experience the Reign of the God. For some 1100 years the Catholic Church which pretty much dominated Christianity used the Latin translation termed the Vulgate which was apparently pretty similar to Jerome's.

In 1516 Desiderius Erasmus put together and published in Basle his first edition of a Greek New Testament drawn from Greek manuscripts available to him with his own Latin translation alongside with the purpose of pointing out to the Roman Church the many and important wrong translations from Greek in the Vulgate. Luther did not follow the Greek nor the Latin translation of Erasmus but rather translated as the verses appear in the Latin Vulgate; the Vulgate has it "nisi quis natus fuerit denuo" and Luther translates the phrase in the Greek the English of which is "unless one might-be-born from-above" into German as "es sei denn, dass jemand von neuem geboren werde" which in English is "unless one would-have-been born anew" just like the Latin Vulgate which we'll see Erasmus had taken such great pains to show is wrong.

God inspired the Apostle John by Holy Spirit to change his phraseology to make it crystal clear throughout 1 John to εκ του θεου γεγεννηται English he has been begotten or born out-of the God as for instance 1 John 3:9 and εξ αυτο γεγεννεται English he has been born out-of Him as in 1 John 2:29. Interestingly, the "Bible scholarly" opinion ignoring the Greek which won the day 400 and again 125 years ago during scholarly proceedings coming up with the KJV and the RV (argument quoted from the infamous Westcott and Hort) overruling the Holy Ghost Author to continue the long

Catholic Church sourced tradition of misrepresenting His phrase γεννηθη ανωθεν as "born-again" instead of as it is literally begotten from-above or born from-above states: "...Nicodemus ought to have wondered how it was possible for anyone to "be born from Heaven" but this he did not say..." Brilliant! So the Scholars explicitly say: "Let's overrule the Logic of God with the logic of Nicodemus." But Jesus says to Nicodemus in verse 10: "Nicodemus, you are the teacher of Israel and you do not know these things?"

Why would anyone overrule God by the understanding of Nicodemus who had snuck in at night to see Jesus? Our Holy Ghost Author wrote the Word in simple precise Common Greek. The scholarly translators deliberately overruled the Author. John 3:7 the Greek Text literally has Jesus saying: "...Do not wonder that I said you must to-be-begotten-from-above!" 3:8 says literally: "So is everyone having-gotten-himself-born out-of the Spirit." The Christian cliché "born-again" nowhere appears in John 3 the God-breathed Greek Text or the corrupt Greek texts.

Does the phrase "born-again" appear in 1Peter 1:23? No, again it does not! Yet the KJV 1:23 says: "...being born-again not of corruptible Seed but of incorruptible by the Word of God..." The NKJV gets the grammar partially correct using a different word saying: "...having-been-regenerated not of corruptible but of incorruptible Seed through the Word of God..." In fact the God-breathed Greek Text says: "...having-gotten-yourselves-up begotten through Word of God..." Again there is no God-breathed indication merely of "again" here but crystal clear statement of getting oneself UPBEGOTTEN or UPBORN through incorruptible Seed. Why would anyone wish to be born-again into the same old corrupt body soul and spirit and situation?

The 1Peter1:3 word you see in your KJV and NKJV as "has begotten... again" is the same Greek verb in 1:23 meaning "Up begotten" but active mood with God the Subject here properly translated has up begotten us or has up seeded us (in English it is the woman who conceives, but in Greek the man supplies the seed or sperm, in this case incorruptible-seed! There is a noun in Greek Text

3824 παλιγγενεσια paliggenesia which literally means "again-become" or "become-again" which appears in Matthew 19:28 and in Titus 3:5 and is translated in both places in the NKJV as "regeneration." The prefix on this word in Greek is palin- which means literally "again." The prefix in Greek for the other two times above in 1Peter1:3, 23 are ana which means up- or upwards- or motion-from-below-upwards.

Notice there is a single Greek letter ν (n) differentiating it from the Greek verb 1080 γενναω gennaoo meaning to beget or seed-to-cause-birth-of. So please after meditating the referenced Scriptures using the literal Holy Ghost meaning consider striking out "born-again" and "begotten-again" and "regenerated" and writing in the margin of your most used Bible in all capital letters "BORN FROM-ABOVE" in JOHN 3 and "UPBEGOTTEN" or "UPBORN" IN 1PETER1. Since you can get from God through the Faith in His promises only what you understand by Revelation He has promised, it is necessary to become diligent to upgrade your understanding supernaturally through meditation.

Let us be mindful that the term "born again", which has been popularized by several prominent ministries, has a ring to it that might never change. We have been so used to addressing this verse as such that it is ingrained in our psyche. However, whether or not we choose to correct this issue, I think it is important for us to know the truth. The term "born again" can easily be mistaken for reincarnation. This was not the plan of God for us to embrace this phraseology in this matter. Born from above indicates that God Himself does the saving. It is a combination of God's sovereignty and man's responsibility for salvation. This might bother some people who feel that they have all of the power to make all of the choices in their life. A deep prayer and study of this issue is important for our spiritual growth.

CHAPTER 13

THERE ARE DIFFERENT KINDS OF LOVE

St. John 21:15-17 "thou lovest me?"

Jesus had a dialogue with Peter about the subject of love. If we were only looking at this passage of Scripture from the English, it would appear as if Jesus was asking Peter an obvious question "do you love me" and He did not hear Peter's response. Jesus kept asking Peter if he loved Him, although Peter responded he was responding with a different definition of love. Jesus was speaking of God's kind of love, whereas Peter was speaking of brotherly love.

Love has many meanings in English, from something that gives a little pleasure ("I loved that movie"). It can describe an intense feeling of affection, an emotion or an emotional state. In ordinary use, it usually refers to interpersonal love. Probably due to its large psychological relevance, love is one of the most common themes in art. The majority of modern movies have a love story and most pop music is about love.

Defining love

There are many forms of love. Love is found in all of human cultures and the type of love that exists in these different cultures portray different views as to what love is. Some have a "real love, and others have a "pseudo love." How do we know which love is real?

There are many different types of love: the love for a soul or mind, love for laws and organizations, love for a body, love for nature, love for food, love for money, love for learning, love for power, love for fame, love for the respect of others, etc. Different people find different types of love more important, and better, than others. Love is abstract, and there are many questions about it.

Interpersonal love

Interpersonal love is love between human beings, and is more sympathetic than the notion of very much liking for another. Although feelings are usually reciprocal, there can also be unrequited love. Interpersonal love is usually found in an interpersonal relationship, such as between family members, friends, and couples. However, people often express love for other people outside of these relationships through compassionate outreach and volunteering.

Some elements that are often present in interpersonal love:

Affection: appreciation of others
Attachment: satisfying basic emotional needs
Reciprocation: if love is mutual
Commitment: a desire to maintain love
Emotional intimacy: sharing emotions and feelings
Kinship: family bonds
Passion: sexual desire
Physical intimacy: sharing of personal space
Self-interest: desiring rewards
Service: desire to help

Companionate vs. passionate

The traditional psychological view sees love as being a combination of companionate love and passionate love. Passionate love is intense longing, and is often accompanied by physiological arousal (shortness of breath, rapid heart rate). Companionate love is affection and a feeling of intimacy not accompanied by physiological arousal.

Sternberg's Triangular Theory of Love

In the triangular theory of love, love is characterized by three elements: intimacy, passion and commitment. Each of these elements can be present in a relationship, producing the following combinations:

Liking includes only one of the love components - intimacy. In this case, liking is not used in a trivial sense. Sternberg says that this intimate liking characterizes true friendships, in which a person feels a bond, warmth, and closeness with another but not intense passion or long-term commitment.

Infatuated love consists solely of passion and is often what is felt as "love at first sight." But without the intimacy and the commitment components of love, infatuated love may disappear suddenly.

Empty love consists of the commitment component without intimacy or passion. Sometimes, a stronger love deteriorates into empty love, in which the commitment remains, but the intimacy and passion have died. In cultures in which arranged marriages are common, relationships often begin as empty love.

Romantic love is a combination of intimacy and passion. Romantic lovers are bonded emotionally (as in liking) and physically through passionate arousal.

Companionate love consists of intimacy and commitment. This type of love is often found in marriages in which the passion has gone out of the relationship, but a deep affection and commitment remain.

Fatuous love has the passion and the commitment components but not the intimacy component. This type of love can be exemplified by a whirlwind courtship and marriage in which a commitment is motivated largely by passion, without the stabilizing influence of intimacy.

Consummate love is the only type of love that includes all three components--intimacy, passion and commitment. Consummate love is the most complete form of love, and it represents the ideal love relationship for which many people strive but which apparently few achieve. Sternberg cautions that maintaining a consummate love may be even harder than achieving it. He stresses the importance of translating the components of love into action. "Without expression," he warns, "even the greatest of loves can die"

Love vs. Insanity?

Studies have shown that mental scans of those in love show a striking resemblance to those with a mental illness. Love creates activity in the same area of the brain that hunger, thirst, and drug cravings create activity in. New love, therefore, could more possibly be physical than emotional.

Over time, this reaction to love mellows, and different areas of the brain are activated, primarily ones involving long-term commitments. Dr. Andrew Newberg, a neuroscientist, suggests that this reaction to love is so similar to that of drugs because without love, humanity would die out.

Ancient Greek

Greek distinguishes several different senses in which the word love is used. For example, ancient Greek has the words philia, eros, agape, storge and xenia. However, with Greek as with many other languages, it has been historically difficult to separate the meanings of these words totally. At the same time the ancient Greek text of the Bible has examples of the verb agapo being used with the same meaning as phileo.

Agape (agápē) means love in modern day Greek. The term S'Agapo means 'I love you' in Greek. The word Agapo is the verb stem, 'I love'. It generally refers to a "pure", ideal type of love rather than the physical attraction suggested by eros. However, there are some examples of agape used to mean the same as eros.

Eros (érōs) is passionate love, with sensual desire and longing. The Greek word 'erota' means 'in love'

Plato refined his own definition. Although eros is initially felt for a person, with contemplation it becomes an appreciation of the beauty within that person, or even becomes appreciation of beauty itself. Eros helps the soul recall knowledge of beauty, and contributes to an understanding of spiritual truth. Lovers and philosophers are all inspired to seek truth by eros.

The conception of Philia (philía), a dispassionate virtuous love, was developed by Aristotle. It includes loyalty to friends, family, and community, and requires virtue, equality and familiarity. Philia is motivated by practical reasons; one or both of the parties benefit from the relationship.

Storge (storgē) is natural affection, like that felt by parents for offspring.

In ancient Greece, the concept of xenia was extremely important. It was an almost ritualized friendship formed between a host and their guest, who could previously be strangers. The host fed and provided quarters for the guest, who was only expected to repay with gratitude. The importance of this can be seen throughout Greek mythology, in particular Homer's Iliad and Odyssey.

Christian

Christians believe that love to God and to other people (God's creation, as they see it) are the two most important things in life (the greatest commandment of God, according to Jesus. See The Gospel of Mark chapter 12, verses 28-34). Saint Augustine summarized this when he wrote "Love God, and do as thou wilt". Paul glorified love as the most important virtue of all in 1 Corinthians, chapter 13. Christians also believe that God felt so much love for man that he sacrificed his son for them. Many Christian theologians see God as the source of love, which is mirrored in humans and their relationships.

In the New Testament, Agape is charitable, selfless, altruistic, and unconditional. It is fatherly love seen as creating goodness in the world, and is reciprocal between believers and God. Also used in the New Testament, Phileo is a human response to something that is found to be delightful. Also known as "brotherly love."

Nomos is devotion to God, and the subjugation of the will before Him and His divine law. In all of this we find a variety of definitions for love. But the greatest act of love was when God sent His Son, Jesus, to die for our sins. There has never been a greater expression of love.

Love Laws from the desk of Professor Smith

Finding Love Again

It is common for couples to feel less loving toward one another. However, we need not let our emotions dictate our responsibility. Our actions often times precede our feelings. If we act loving and kind toward our spouse, or even someone who has hurt us, we will eventually allow the feelings of positivism to flourish. I believe fantasy love is an emotional kick that we all look forward to getting all the time, because we see it in the movies or read about it in magazines. But the truth of the matter is that this type of love doesn't last.

When our neurotransmitters are firing everything is great. Our adrenaline is pumping and we feel like a million bucks. But when the fabulous emotional high is gone then the reality begins to stare us in the face. Do we have the courage and the dedication to stand up to the challenge of less exciting times? This is a question that must be asked before couples are thinking about a serious relationship. A real relationship is about sacrifice. It is about give and take. It isn't easy. As a matter of fact, it's hard. But with the help of the Lord it is something that can be done. Remember the benefits outweigh the deficits. The good will outweigh the bad.

Women Talk

Women generally speak in opposites, i.e. emotional language. When they say, "You don't have to buy me anything" you can interpret this as saying, "You better buy me something or else." Women generally want you to initiate the idea and to carry out the

action on your own. When we show this motivation to please our partner they are more likely to embrace our efforts.

Men Talk

That's the problem, we don't talk! I often wonder why we are so "stoic." We generally don't want do deal with every little bit of information. Some reports show that men speak about 2,000 words a day while women speak about 10,000 a day. This may shed some light for the women. Men generally talk less but do more.

Problems with choosing in a relationship

I've heard too often women complain about how their man isn't being the man that they would like him to be. They ask me how they can make him become a man. But the question that should be asked is, have they chosen a weak person in order to feel strong? Too often women and men choose a weak mate, and then complain that their mate isn't strong enough for them. They choose a weak person because they believe that the weak person can't hurt them. However, the real question remains. What happens when the weak person gets strong? If the weak person gets strong then he or she may not need you anymore for strength.

Too often we are weak so weak persons don't choose someone who is strong and capable of handling life's challenges instead we choose someone who is weaker in order for us to feel better about ourselves. It is like you feeling upset about making $5.00 dollars an hour, but you feel better when you know that your friend is only making $3.00. The goal for us is to first become strong and grounded so that we can make better choices. We generally choose from our current state of being. We know who is too much to handle and who is just good enough for the ride.

Control Freaks

Control freaks often times do so out of insecurity. They feel threatened and so they strong arm their partner in order to feel safe themselves. If this be the case, then find a way to make them feel more secure about themselves. This is simply a cry for reassurance. Let them know that this type of behavior is not tolerated.

Honoring Your Parents

This may come as a shock to you, but your parents are not always right. We should never Honor our parents if it dishonors God. If our parents are wrong then they are wrong. Honoring them doesn't mean we have to support what they are doing. Remember God is first. What God says goes. This commandment tells us that we should treat them with respect; it doesn't mean justify every act that they do.

Let Them Talk

People are going to talk about you no matter what you say or do. This is a part of human behavior. So let them talk. Get a grip. I believe that you should first analyze what is being said. Most criticism has its basis in reality whether we like it or not. People do see what we generally don't. So we should think about the attack on us before we react. If we know that we are clean then just ignore them. They have nothing else better to do but get in your business, because their life is boring and they don't have enough business of their own.

Don't Get Caught Up in the Fantasy

Truth oftentimes interferes with reality. We get stuck on wanting to be something that we're not. We believe a lie because there is a sense of security in believing a lie. Stop living in a fantasy world. Get a hold of yourself. This is not the life that you are to be living. Seek God for guidance. You are wasting you time. Remember a frog that jumps in boiling water will jump out, but when that same frog is in regular water that is being warmed, it will warm to a boil and the frog won't do a thing. It is a slow process that gets us caught up.

We get the hype from movies and Hollywood. We think that we are something that we are not. We are being brain washed by the media and the oppression of the world's influence. Embrace the truth, whether it is about love, religion, etc. Seek the truth.

CHAPTER 14

OTHER TONGUES/LANGUAGES!!

Book of Acts, chapter 2.

What Other Tongues?

And when the day of Pentecost was fully come, they were all with one accord in one place. And suddenly there came a sound from heaven as of a rushing mighty wind, and it filled all the house where they were sitting. And there appeared unto them cloven tongues like as of fire, and it sat upon each of them. And they were all filled with the Holy Ghost, and began to speak with other tongues, as the Spirit gave them utterance.

And there were dwelling at Jerusalem Jews, devout men, out of every nation under heaven. Now when this was noised abroad, the multitude came together, and was confounded, because that every man heard them speak in his own language. And they were all amazed and marveled, saying one to another, Behold, are not all these which speak Galileans? And how hear we every man in our own tongue, wherein we were born? Parthian, and Medes, and Elamites, and the dwellers in Mesopotamia, and in Judaea, and Cappadocia, in Pontus, and Asia, Phrygia, and Pamphylia, in Egypt, and in the parts of Libya about Cyrene, and strangers of Rome, Jews and proselytes, Cretes and Arabians, we do hear them speak in our tongues the wonderful works of God. - Acts 2:1-18

The spectacular event described here was a one time, unprecedented, profound manifestation of Yahweh's power in the sight of men. Taken in perspective as to the occasion it marked, the birth of Yeshua's Church in the world, it was arguably an even more notable event than the series of miracles by which Yahweh delivered the Israelites out of Pharaoh's Egypt or the flood of Noah's day.

I'd like to narrow the focus down to a simple issue, and I think most would find what I'm about to propose credible, even though it is not at all consistent with common teachings. The question is what language(s) did these initial recipients of the Holy Spirit speak? I count 15 distinct ethnic groups listed in verses 9 through 11. I can't explicitly say that each of these represents a unique language or not, though that does seem to be the author's intent. In any event, there was clearly quite an array of different native languages represented by the group of witnesses to this event. Nevertheless, I'd like to propose that it is likely that the group of disciples who, with cloven tongues of fire appearing on them, were not moved by the Spirit to speak in 15 different languages, nor twelve, six or even two. Rather, it seems to me that they spoke in one language only, and that language was what Paul later called the tongues of angels.

You may be thinking, 'But, but...there were 15 different ethnic groups there who all heard them in their own language!' coupled, perhaps, with, 'What kind of nut are you, anyway!' But let's examine the text closely, for in it we find nothing that says they SPOKE in the languages of all these different people, but rather that those people HEARD in their own language. Is that splitting hairs? You may (in fact, you must) judge for yourself, but please hear me out.

First of all, I'm not about to tell you that God is not able to supernaturally give someone the ability to speak in another language which they have not learned. I don't believe that myself, but I know of no Biblical record of any such thing, either, the possibility of that being the case in Acts 2 notwithstanding. There are, however, many cases recorded in the Scriptures of people speaking in an unknown tongue upon receiving the Holy Spirit, but these all point to a language that is otherwise unknown in the world, the tongues of angels. In fact, from this point on, the book of Acts consistently depicts this as a normal manifestation by those who receive the Spirit, as well as evidence of the same to others. The point is that the Biblical record shows substantial precedent of the Spirit giving people utterance in the same angelic language, but there is no specific record of the Spirit giving people utterance in diverse human languages. (I trust that someone will advise me if I'm overlooking something on the latter point.)

Now let me turn your attention to the other side of this equation. On one hand we have the 120 or so disciples who were speaking as the newly poured out Holy Spirit gave them utterance, and on the other we have thousands of ethnically diverse Jews nearby who all heard them speak in their own language of the wonderful works of God. It is this fact that has caused most people to believe that the Spirit given utterances of that occasion were a supernaturally given ability to speak in unlearned human languages. It doesn't say that, though.

A lot of people would agree that such would at least be an exception to the normal manifestation of speaking in tongues. Others maintain that speaking in tongues as described in the Bible IS speaking in an otherwise unknown human language, and, even though it doesn't really say that, base their arguments on this passage.

Again, it says they HEARD what was being spoken in their own language, but all it says of those speaking is that they spoke in other tongues as the Spirit gave them utterance. Turning again to Scriptural precedent, Paul lists and discusses a common ministry gift of the Spirit known as interpretation of tongues in chapters 12 and 14 of his first epistle to the Corinthians. The net result of the operation of this gift is the same as prophesying, the difference being that (properly conducted) one person speaks a message in tongues while another translates it for the rest of the congregation. The person who interprets hears the message in the tongues of angels, but by the working of the same Spirit, is given understanding of it as though spoken in their own native tongue.

While it would be a mistake to portray this event as ordinary, it did mark the beginning of new things that shortly thereafter became common amongst the believers. Two of those things were speaking and interpreting the tongues of angels. It seems far more plausible that these 120 or so disciples experienced the same thing that others who followed them did upon receiving the Spirit -- speaking in the tongues of angels -- than that they manifested a one time miracle of speaking in a dozen or more languages simultaneously. Likewise, it seems more likely that the chosen audience for the ministry that was going forth at that moment were given ears to hear, so to speak, by the same operation of the Spirit Paul discussed in 1 Corinthians 12 and 14 than the alternative.

Judging by various other translations, the KJV rendition of Acts 2:6 is a bit misleading. It reads, "Now when this was noised abroad, the multitudes came together, and were confounded, because that every man heard them speak in his own language." I verified this through several others, but I'll use the NAS version as sufficient to illustrate this point:

And when the day of Pentecost had come, they were all together in one place. And suddenly there came from heaven a noise like a violent, rushing wind, and it filled the whole house where they were sitting. And there appeared to them tongues as of fire distributing themselves, and they rested on each one of them. And they were all filled with the Holy Spirit and began to speak with other tongues, as the Spirit was giving them utterance.

Now there were Jews living in Jerusalem, devout men, from every nation under heaven. And when this sound occurred, the multitude came together, and were bewildered, because they were each one hearing them speak in his own language. And they were amazed and marveled, saying, "Why, are not all these who are speaking Galileans? "And how is it that we each hear {them} in our own language to which we were born?" - Acts 2:1-8 (NAS)

What I'd like to call your attention to is where it says "this sound" in verse 6. What sound? There are two options given: In verse 2 there was the noise coming from heaven like a violent, rushing wind, and there was the voices of those speaking with other tongues as the Spirit gave them utterance. The most natural reading of the passage indicates that the noise in verse 2 gives way to the sound of their voices in verse 4, which is also the latter of the two. Also, the word translated as 'sound' in verse 4 is most commonly rendered as 'voice' in the New Testament and the remainder of verse 6 strongly indicates that the 'sound' that caught their attention was the sound of the disciples' voices speaking in strange tongues.

Try to picture this scenario: The voices of the disciples speaking as the Spirit gave them utterance was significant enough to catch the attention of a very large and diverse crowd. On top of that, the gathering crowd was bewildered, amazed, and marveling at what they were witnessing, and, naturally, they were all conversing with one another while this is going on. Others mocked them, speculating that they were drunk. Can you picture this? What do you see? I see a riotous gathering of several thousand people.

Let's consider these crowd reactions. If someone spoke perfect, coherent English to you, would you think they were drunk? Everyone knows that one of the most prominent indications of being drunk is that it impedes your speech. If someone started talking in a language that didn't sound like any language I'd ever heard, I might think they were drunk, but not if they were speaking clearly in my own language. I might be amazed and bewildered if I knew for a fact that they didn't naturally speak my language, but I wouldn't think them drunk.

This crowd demonstrated two very contrary reactions. While some marveled in amazement at the prophesying they heard, others thought they were drunk and mocked them. We know that by the time that day finished, about three thousand souls of the devout Jews in Jerusalem at that time were added to Yeshua's Church out of that crowd, but we also know that there were plenty of scoffers there, too. Each may draw their own conclusions, but I just don't find it reasonable to conclude that those who thought they were drunk and mocked them heard them speaking of the wonderful works of God in their own language like the others did. I propose that some had ears to hear and heard, which in this case would have been the first example of interpretation of tongues recorded, and would be on par with the profound degree that speaking in the tongues of angels was manifested at the same time.

One more thing that I'd like to ask before I conclude is this: Have you ever been involved in a small group where several different conversations are going simultaneously? Even in a small gathering, it can get pretty hard to distinguish one voice from another. With that in mind, go back to the scenario described in Acts 2. I've tried to feature the small group of disciples gathered together and loudly speaking in numerous different languages to this crowd, and I just don't see how those assembled could have discerned one language from another in such a setting. That picture actually reminds me of the confounding of languages Yahweh did to obstruct the construction of the city and tower of Babel. (Not that it wouldn't be possible, it just seems that being able to hear their own language in the midst of all this would require a more significant miracle than being enabled by the Spirit to interpret a single language being spoken by the small group of disciples.)

In conclusion, I recognize that what I've said here is arguable. I always search for relevance when I consider things like this, and the relevance here doesn't directly apply to everyone. For those who argue that the gift of speaking in tongues is nothing more than a supernatural ability to speak in a foreign human language, it is pertinent. If what I have presented here is arguable, doctrines such as this that are built on the same passage of Scripture are without foundation. That speaking in the tongues of angels (not foreign languages) is a common, ordinary manifestation of being filled with the Holy Spirit is well documented elsewhere in the Scriptures.

Acts 2 only represents the beginning of this new thing that was given to God's people nearly 2,000 years ago, which is why it is important to dispense with false or unfounded conclusions being drawn from it. At the very least, one should at least recognize that the fact that this passage only says that they spoke as the Spirit gave them utterance and that the audience heard in their own language. It does not explicitly resolve how this was accomplished, and it most certainly does not form a foundation for a doctrine that portrays speaking in tongues as spoken of often in the Scriptures as speaking in a foreign human language and nothing more.

CHAPTER 15

"TOUCH NOT!' "ARE YOU SURE?"

Colossians 2:21 . . . touch not, taste not.

Once again Paul uses the difficult but important catchword stoicheia, translated "basic principles," to call attention to his opponent's preoccupation with the four basic elements of earth (see 2:8), which make up the very things not handled, not tasted, not touched. From the beginning of his letter, Paul has underscored the importance of relating the material world to the spiritual: the one should always bear witness to the other. Indeed, in the next passage Paul will again admonish his readers to understand the "earthly" in terms of the "heavenly" (3:1-4). This integration of spirit and heaven with matter and earth provides the foundation for Paul's ethical program (3:5--4:1), where the moral emphasis falls on transformed relationships rather than the regulations of ascetic piety.

Perhaps it is prudent to point out that Paul's concern is not so much that a Christian's spirituality is abundantly "worldly"; rather, he is concerned that the rigors of Christian devotion not be viewed as means for acquiring God's grace. In fact, our devotion to God should include a measure of self-denial (compare Mk 8:34-38) coupled with a resolve not to conform to the norms and values of secular culture. However, these virtues are the fruit of participating with Christ in the salvation of God. Our rejection of middle-class materialism and our embracing of a simple lifestyle, then, constitute a positive response to Christ's lordship rather than a negative response to a world we suppose is inherently evil. The Rules of Wrong Religion (2:20-21)

Paul reminds his readers of an accepted fact (ei indic): you died with Christ to the basic principles of this world. The moral response of true religion does not consist of codes having to do with earth's elements, even if we are denying ourselves the use of those elements (compare 2:8). In fact, Paul will go on in chapter 3 to describe the moral life of Christian faith in terms of codes of human virtue and relationships.

Colossi's spiritual empire has been teaching that spiritual maturity is reflected more by the believer's self-centered asceticism than by transformed relationships. Logically, Christians who place greatest priority on other worldly experiences will tend to deny the value of this world, even (ironically) to emphasize its denial. In Colosse, where some equate spiritual maturity with otherworldly visions of angels, certain religious behaviors give concrete expression to their world-denying orientation. Thus, it is claimed, the mature believer will abstain from certain foods (2:16) or activities (compare 3:5-11): Do not handle! Do not taste! Do not touch! Such are those who are not yet liberated from the basic principles by affirming in practice the lordship of Christ over earth and its elements.

Paul may well be mocking actual prohibitions used at Colosse, probably to express religious (do not taste certain foods) and social (do not touch certain people) commitments. While the background of these prohibitions is not known, it is not difficult to find similar sayings in both Jewish and pagan literature of Paul's day (for these see O'Brien 1983:149-50). Again, the problem for Paul is not really the idea of religious asceticism; he even encourages certain ascetic practices on occasion (compare 1 Corinthians 7). Rather, his primary concern is what religious motivation prompts this lifestyle and whether it ultimately enhances the believer's relationship with Christ and neighbor. Clearly, he believes that submission to these moral codes tends to denigrate Christ's redemptive work and promote enmity between believers. They simply do not have much spiritual cash value.

The verb submit (dogmatizo, from which we get "dogmatic" and "dogma") in this context means to submit to certain official decrees or legal obligations, presumably in order to be freed of some debt or to keep from being indebted (and worse). If this debt is owed to something or someone other than Christ, then such devotion is wrong-headed. Further, we may presume from Paul's teaching that to encourage legalism, as such codes surely do, is to discourage the grace that is available to all who have died with Christ. The Results of Wrong Religion (2:22-23)

Paul further justifies his criticism of Christian asceticism through a twofold appeal to common sense. First of all, he says, any rule of faith that is based on prohibitions such as those listed in verse 21 could not possibly be effective, because they are based on things (such as food) that perish. Why determine the eternal by the temporal? This seems as foolish as idolatry, which substitutes what is created for its Creator. Further, perishable items lack eschatological value, since they belong to the world order that will perish at Christ's return. Second, this same ascetic rule of faith is based on human commands and teachings. Not only are the prohibited commodities perishable, but

their disposition is determined by human patterns ("dogma") of consumption (such as etiquette), whether ascetic or hedonistic.

To conclude his polemic against the champions of Colossian philosophy, Paul returns to his initial concern (2:4) over any purportedly wise teaching in a cultural environment that responds favorably to "fine-sounding arguments." When one scratches the surface of such teaching and finds that it fails to insist on the Lord Christ's singular importance, Paul asserts, the church must condemn it as "hollow and deceptive" (2:8). Any Christ less version of truth has no redemptive value. Likewise, the regulations of ascetic piety have no redemptive value because they too are based on human commands and teachings (2:21-22; compare 2:8) rather than on Christ. They too have an appearance of wisdom (compare 2:4) in a religious environment where self-denial is honored, but in reality they lack any value in restraining sensual indulgence.

Paul's final word is "flesh" (sarx), which the NIV takes in its pejorative sense, "sin nature." When coupled with his earlier phrase treatment of the body (soma), Paul's criticism is ironical: a legalistic concern to abstain from bodily indulgence will result in a concern for the physical that is actually "fleshly," lacking in any spiritual value. Not only does legalism demote the importance of divine grace, it also focuses primary attention on the physical "what" rather than the theological "why." In this sense self-denial is actually counterproductive for faith.

Perhaps in reaction to a culture dominated by impersonal technology, today we hunger more than ever for a personal experience with God. Yet because of technology, we have also come to expect the spectacular even in the ordinary routine of life. Technology makes life easier for us. More and more Christians seek spectacular experiences of God; we demand "signs and wonders" that will make our lives easier. God is just another name for technology. Paul would break no compromise with any religious philosophy that promotes a spectacular brilliance or a mystical experience as the badge of an abundant spirituality (see 2:16-18). He would interpret our current emphasis on personal, dramatic religious experiences as a threat to the centrality of the congregation's relationship with Christ and the spiritual disciplines that fortify that relationship (2:19).

This passage is also an important corrective to any version of Christianity that is world-denying (2:20-23). If Christ is Lord over the created order (1:15-18), his people should be actively engaged in transforming all things to accord with the Creator's good intentions for them. Ironically, believers who legalistically follow codes that deny or limit interest in the material or sensual are routinely seduced into another kind of sensual indulgence--one that replaces selfless devotion to Jesus with self-centered concern over the proper handling of those very natural elements, he rules as Lord.

CHAPTER 16

THE LOVE OF MONEY = ALL EVIL?

I Timothy 6:10 all sorts of evil

The Christian View of Money

The real issue is in the correct translation. Paul's argument would correctly show that the love of money will lead to all sorts of evil. But all evil can't have its origin in money. Money only existed a few thousand years ago. In many places of the world, trade was the way in which people got what they needed. They would grow a product and then trade it for another. All evil isn't connected with money. Some evil is religious ideology. Other kinds of evil like sexual perversion, hatred for others, etc., aren't necessarily tied into money. The translation of the King James Version didn't do this passage justice. Although I personally like this Version, you cannot escape searching the Hebrew and the Greek text for greater accuracy.

Paul tells us that the Christian's goal with respect to material things is godliness with contentment. Godliness in Paul's vocabulary means the genuine Christian life, a faith-relationship with God and a new way of life. Contentment is a Pauline word in the New Testament (2 Corinthians 9:8; compare Phil 4:11). It had a prominent place in Stoic philosophy, where it defined an attitude of "self-sufficiency," meaning detachment or independence from things or possessions. Contentment came from within. Paul approved of this idea but naturally supplied a Christian basis for it: "I have learned to be content whatever the circumstances. . . . I can do everything through him who gives me strength" (Phil 4:11, 13). Thus for Paul the Christian goal is a genuine relationship with God, our source of contentment, and a healthy detachment from material things. This combination is great gain. In contrast to 6:5, gain here is measured according to spiritual rather than material value. Eternal benefits are surely promised, but the focus is on how the believer with this healthy perspective can avoid the many pitfalls of greed in the present life.

To ground his view of contentment, Paul draws on Old Testament wisdom. Both Job 1:21 and Ecclesiastes 5:15 expound the principle that material things belong only to this world. Things have no lasting value and provide no eternal advantage. Therefore one's contentment cannot stem from things. Human contact with the material world begins at birth and terminates at death. But Christian hope takes the believer beyond the material limit to a boundless eternity, and logically, then, eternal values must shape our view of temporal things.

This leads to a question: For the Christian how much is enough? Paul's principle implies a standard of material sufficiency that is minimal indeed. Food and clothing ought to be enough. While Paul may be quoting popular philosophy, it is far more likely that he is drawing from the model of Christ (Mt 6:25-34; Luke 12:16-21). He does not say anything negative about living above this minimum standard, though he will teach that life at a higher material level carries with it heavy obligations. But he does say that real contentment and material prosperity have nothing to do with one another. And acquisitiveness has nothing to do with godliness.

How can the Christian learn to be content with simple living? Certainly not by accepting the standards set by this world. Paul suggests that an eternal perspective and an attitude of detachment toward things are prerequisites. As an eternal perspective develops, dependence on things material will decline.

Origin of Money-

Money has become such a routine part of our lives... Its origin is rarely considered or understood. So what is money? Money is a claim, clear and simple. Whereas money is often defined as a store of value, medium of exchange or a measure of value, these are only its uses, not what it is. Money is a claim for something of value.

The original groups of hunter-gatherers didn't need money as they provided only for themselves. Eventually they came to trade with other groups by direct barter, i.e. one to one, without money. Later, trading became more convenient with the use of indirect barter, i.e. trading into a common third party commodity which is then traded for the intended item. Practically every medium such as sea shells, bananas, cattle, land and metal has been used for the third party commodity which becomes known as money.

With the advent of indirect barter, i.e. the use of money, trading was made easier and commerce was born. As man's wealth developed, gold and silver became the most accepted medium for indirect barter. Freed from a medium that did not rot or walk away, man began to accumulate wealth. As the goldsmiths had already built strong rooms, people stored their gold with the goldsmith and received a warehouse receipt. After people learned to accept the warehouse receipt in lieu of the actual gold or silver, the depositors found it was easier to get several smaller warehouse receipts. As these small warehouse receipts became popular they were used exclusively as they still represented stored value. Then over time, the goldsmiths became bankers and the warehouse receipts became banknotes.

Unfortunately, the bankers soon realized that the people rarely redeemed the gold and they began to issue duplicate warehouse receipts. Eventually this fraud of fractional reserve banking was legalized as the Federal Reserve System by the government for their own unconstitutional motives.

In conclusion we have established that money itself did not exist in the days of old. It cannot be the root of all evil, because evil existed before money did. We have money and we are to use the money for the purpose the God has given us in our lives. Money is the means, but not the end. It is the product by which we use to obtain and to advance. It should not be worshipped or hoarded as if it held the greatest of all positions in our lives. We are to put God and others over our desire for money. We should not look upon people that do not have it as if they are less important than us. If we have it we need to share it and help those who are in hard situations. Money can be a good thing. It can help lots of people and do great work for the Lord. If we keep our priorities straight we will be a blessing to many.

Words on Wealth

You've heard it said that money is the root of all evil, right? Wrong! Paul was addressing Timothy, as he was preparing him for public ministry. I Tim. 6: 10 "For the love of money (and all it buys) placed before the love of God (in reality) is the root of all kinds of evil."

Did you catch that? Let me reread it. A clear distinction must be made between THE LOVE of money and money itself. Let this truth sink deep into your spirit. God is not anti-money, or anti-wealth, He is anti-money WORSHIP. He has helped us to identify that money love (worship) is the root of all kinds of evil. In fact, as we have discussed before, God's plan is that we are healthy, wealthy, and wise in this world -- as a testimony of His greatness, power, and glory to come.

Wealth is NOT the only measuring stick of our blessing from God. Wealth is an indication that a godly man has his house in order but not a guarantee of spirituality. The world is full of rich men and women who are lost spiritually. On the other hand, the majority of the world's people are both lost and poor (like India and China). This means that we cannot boast in our wealth, but rather, as Christians we are to learn to be content in whatever station of life we find ourselves.

My point is that the LOVE of money is the critical factor in determining if money is used for good or evil, from God's perspective. What about Mother Teresa you ask? She was certainly a blessed woman without any wealth at all. True. If only we had a planet full of Mother Teresa's. The reality is that she has answered a special call from God to live among the poor, and to minister the love of God unencumbered by the distractions of possessions. There are others called to minister to the middle class, who teach that fulfillment is not to be found in keeping up with the Joneses. There are others who are called to minister to the rich, famous, and powerful by demonstrating that money can be used to restore godly principles back into a culture.

The bottom line is that money, like technology, is spiritually neutral. It can be used for good or evil. God always deals with the heart and the motives of the use of money. If the motives are pure then the fruit can be very good. Let's stop loving things and start loving people. That is the measure of true wealth!

Richest countries in the world

Based on these and many other statistics, we are a rich nation. Even the "Poor" in America is rich compared to other countries of the world.

Richest Countries in the World		
Rank	Country	GDP - per capita
1	Luxembourg	$ 55,100
2	Norway	$ 37,800
3	United States	$ 37,800
4	San Marino	$ 34,600
5	Switzerland	$ 32,700
6	Denmark	$ 31,100
7	Iceland	$ 30,900
8	Austria	$ 30,000
9	Canada	$ 29,800
10	Ireland	$ 29,600
11	Belgium	$ 29,100
12	Australia	$ 29,000
13	Netherlands	$ 28,600
14	Japan	$ 28,200
15	United Kingdom	$ 27,700
16	France	$ 27,600
17	Germany	$ 27,600
18	Finland	$ 27,400
19	Monaco	$ 27,000
20	Sweden	$ 26,800

Source: CIA World Fact book

Poorest Countries in the World		
Rank	Country	GDP - per ca
1	East Timor	$ 500
2	Somalia	$ 500
3	Sierra Leone	$ 500
4	Malawi	$ 600
5	Tanzania	$ 600
6	Burundi	$ 600
7	Congo, Republic of the	$ 700
8	Congo, Democratic Republic of the	$ 700
9	Comoros	$ 700
10	Eritrea	$ 700
11	Ethiopia	$ 700
12	Afghanistan	$ 700
13	Niger	$ 800
14	Yemen	$ 800
15	Madagascar	$ 800
16	Guinea-Bissau	$ 800
17	Zambia	$ 800
18	Kiribati	$ 800
19	Nigeria	$ 900
20	Mali	$ 900

When I preached throughout West Africa I was heart broken to see the poor condition many of the people lived in. We are so blessed in this country. We should thank God every day, because even the poor in America are among the richest in the World. When you consider that a typical poor person in the U.S. has three televisions, cell phones and a brand new car, we have to rethink what is poor. The fact that we have street lights, and paved roads is a sign of wealth. Please understand me, there are poor people in this Country, but the statement I'm poor" is overstated. The Bible says that the "poor will be with us always". Therefore, let us continue to support missions and the work that the Church is obligated to do.

CHAPTER 17

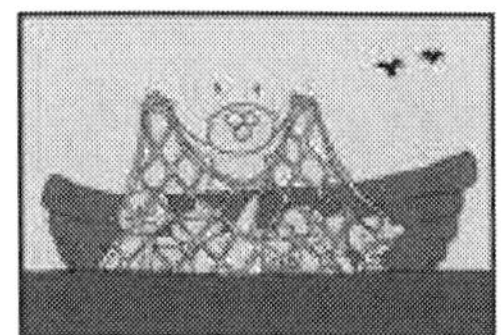

ALL MEN ARE DRAWN UNTO HIM?

John 12:32 If I be lifted up I will draw all men

The literal Koine Greek translation would read "if I be lifted up I will drag all sorts of men unto me." Does this mean that every single man, woman, boy and girl is drawn unto him? This must be if we see this Scripture as such. This would indicate that If Jesus were lifted up, and we know that He was, then He would draw everyone unto

Himself, thus making everyone His? This is one of the strong points of the "Inclusionist Philosophers" theory. This is why people like Carlton Pierson, accept the teaching that all people eventually go to God. However, this view point is not supported by Scripture. As we have discovered with the passage on money being the root to all evil, we find a weakness in the translation. The bible translation should have read, as it does more accurately, "all sorts of people."

The Greek expressions rendered "all" and "everyone" in these verses is inflected forms of the word pas. As shown in Vine's Expository Dictionary of New Testament Words (London, 1962, Vol. I, p. 46), pas can also mean "every kind or variety." So, in the above verses, instead of "all," the expression "every kind of" could be used; or "all sorts of." The contexts in which this verse is written would imply all sorts of men, not every single man. If all men were saved then we would have to do away with all of the Scriptures making references to Hell.

Christian Universalism Statement of Faith

What is Christian Universalism? Christian universalism is a belief in the simple Bible truth that Jesus Christ is the "Lamb who takes away the sin of the world." He is the promised Messiah of whom the prophets of the Old Covenant foresaw; He is the Savior of the world; He is the "Second Adam;" through Whom all mankind will be restored to God's original image; He is the only way to the Father; the only begotten Son of God; and that there is no other way to everlasting, "aionian" life but through Him. We believe He is King and judge of the universe, and owner of all Creation, and that His purpose for the ages (aions) are to bring all things under His government and reconciled with Himself.

We believe that in His substitutionary death and resurrection He became the "Lamb who takes away the sin of the world." As Christ Himself said, "If I be lifted up (crucified) I will draw all men to me" (as also prophesied in Psalm 22). His Name is the One before which every man; woman and child, from all of human history will bow before and declare that He is Lord. At that day, the prophesied "restoration of all things" shall come to pass, and of the increase of His government and peace there shall be no end.

This view is also known as Ultimate reconciliation or Universal Salvation, which is a very different thing than Unitarian Universalism. Carlton Pearson as well as others has accepted this early heretical teaching as orthodox Christian teaching. Yet this teaching has been condemned throughout most of the early Church Fathers.

There is also a teaching associated with this organization that believe that Satan himself and all of the other fallen angels will accept Jesus and avoid eternal punishment. A simple response to these allegations is to study the word of God. To examine the Hebrew and Koine Greek Scriptures as well as take a few courses in Hermeneutics. In addition we must learn to pray for these people who have embraced a lie. Why would we need to evangelize if everyone was to go to heaven eventually?

CHAPTER 18

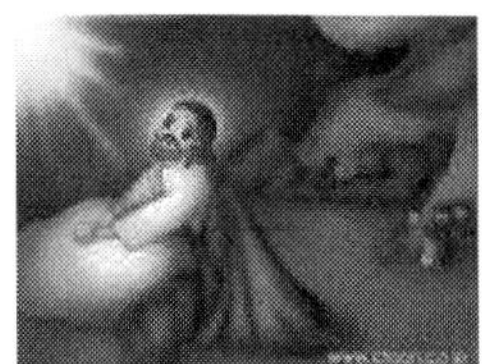

GOD CANNOT DO EVERYTHING!

2 Tim 2:13 (Nor has He seen everything)

"If we believe not, yet he abideth faithful: he cannot deny himself." God sees all and knows all, but He will not do all, because He cannot do what is against His nature. It isn't as if He is impotent and doesn't have the power to do, He will not do because He is God. God is faithful to His word.

God sees and knows all things.	God neither sees nor knows all things?
Job 42:2 No thought can be withholden from thee. Psalm 44:21 For he knoweth the secrets of the heart. Psalm 139:7-8 Whither shall I flee from thy presence? If I ascend up into heaven, thou art there; if I make my bed in hell, behold, thou art there. Proverbs 15:3 The eyes of the Lord are in every place. Jeremiah 16:17 For mine eyes are upon all their ways: they are not hid from my face, neither is their iniquity hid from mine eyes. Jeremiah 23:24 Can any hide himself in secret places that I shall not see him? saith the Lord. Do not I fill heaven and earth? Acts 1:24 Thou, Lord, which knoweth the hearts of all men.	Genesis 3:8 And Adam and his wife hid themselves from the presence of the Lord, amongst the trees of the garden. Genesis 4:14 Behold, thou hast driven me out this day from the face of the earth; and from thy face shall I be hid. Genesis 4:16 And Cain went out from the presence of the LORD, and dwelt in the land of Nod, on the east of Eden. Genesis 11:5 And the Lord came down to see the city and the town. Genesis 18:9 And they said unto him, Where is Sarah thy wife? And he said, Behold, in the tent. Genesis 18:17 And the LORD said, Shall I hide from Abraham that thing which I do? Genesis 18:20-21 And the Lord said, Because the cry of Sodom and Gomorrah is great, and because their sin is

very grievous, I will go down now and see whether they have done altogether according to the cry of it, which is come unto me; and, if not, I will know.

Genesis 22:12

For now I know that thou fearest God, seeing thou hast not withheld thy son, thine only son from me.

Numbers 22:9

And God came unto Balaam, and said, What men are these with thee?

Deuteronomy 8:2

God led thee these forty years in the wilderness ... to know what in thine heart.

Deuteronomy 13:3

The Lord your God proveth you, to know whether ye love the Lord your God.

2 Chronicles 32:31

God left him, to try him that he might know all that was in his heart.

Job 1:7, 2:2

And the Lord said unto Satan, Whence comest thou? Then Satan answered the Lord, and said, from going to and fro in the earth, and from walking up and down in it.

Hosea 8:4

	They have set up kings, but not by me: they have made princes, and I knew it not.

What we see in the "Haven't seen category" simply is God communicating with man on our level. He writes to us often in anthropomorphic terms so that we could better identify with Him. He is a personal God and wants a personal relationship with us. We read as if He doesn't know, yet He knows, but He wants us to do our part. God wants a relationship with us.

God cannot do what will go against His nature. A righteous God cannot be involved in unrighteousness. God cannot do anything evil. He, through His sovereignty may allow evil, but He is not directly responsible for it. God has allowed evil, through the use of secondary agents. More on this subject will be in the chapter God and evil. In regards to things God has not seen:

He has never seen a cancer He couldn't heal
He has never seen a sinner He couldn't save
He has never seen a bout of depression He couldn't restore
He has never seen a weakness He couldn't make strong

These are just a few things that God has never seen.

CHAPTER 19

NOT IN THE ORIGINAL TEXT

I John 5:7-8 not in the original

As we start this section, let us be aware that the original bible, i.e. the Greek manuscript had no periods or commas. All of the documents were written bunched together. For example interpret the following:

GOD IS NOWHERE

Which is it? Is it God is now here, or God is no where? This is the issue that faces many of the Bible translators. Every Scripture runs into the other. The way in which the translators interpret is by looking at the context. The context helps us to understand what would be the most likely passage.

The bible itself has no errors. But what the Bible does have is what is called copyist errors. Because the authors were writing on rocks, in dark caves, with feathers and a small candle, often times in smelly, wet dungeons, it was possible to make a copyist error. They did not have Kinko's or fax machines to get reprints of the original autographs out to the rest of the world. They had to rely on rewriting the material. In addition there was a rush job done with the King James Version, due to political pressure, thus some side notes were added into the text. This passage was an example of a side note that was accidentally added to the text.

1 John 5:7-8 (KJV) For there are three that bear record in heaven, the Father, the Word, and the Holy Ghost: and these three are one. {8} And there are three that bear witness in earth, the Spirit, and the water, and the blood: and these three agree in one.

(NIV) 7 For there are three that testify: 8 the Spirit, the water and the blood; and the three are in agreement.

(NASV) 7 For there are three that testify: 8 the Spirit and the water and the blood; and the three are in agreement.

(1901 ASV) 7 And it is the Spirit that beareth witness, because the Spirit is the truth. 8 For there are three who bear witness, the Spirit, and the water, and the blood: and the three agree in one.

(NAB-Roman Catholic) 7 So there are three that testify 8 the Spirit, the water, and the blood, and the three are of one accord.

(NKJV) Footnote - NU-Text and M-Text omit the words from in heaven (verse 7) through on earth (verse 8). Only four or five very late manuscripts contain these words in Greek. (The NKJV is a notorious version with their doubt casting footnotes which have the same devastating effect as if they just mutilated the text itself. Do you see they claim only four or five late manuscripts have the verse in them? We saw a lot more evidence than 4 or 5 which means they are deceiving their readers which means the NKJV also qualifies as a false version.)

Corrupted Manuscripts

These verses are corrupted in the following manuscripts:

Sinaiticus -	FourthCentury
Sinaiticus -	Fourth Century
Alexandrines -	Fifth Century

These three manuscripts are the primary manuscripts where 1 John 5:7-8 have been corrupted. There are many other later manuscripts which are ancillary to these three because they were copied from them. Like begets like and when you copy from corrupted manuscripts the lineage of corruption will continue. 1 John 5:7-8 has been attacked by the pro modern version crowd as being a scribal addition later on in years. However, 1 John 5:7-8 is found in the Old Latin Vulgate and Greek Vulgate (90-150 A.D.), plus the Syriac Peshiito (150 A.D.) It is also found in many First Century church lectionaries.

Dr. John Overall, who was one of the King James translators, was a scholar in the teachings of the early Church Fathers. His contribution concerning 1 John 5:7 was vital since manuscript evidence was lacking because of the Alexandrian school where it was mutilated. He knew that the early church fathers had referenced those verses quite frequently. The modern version proponents only look to

Vaticanus and Sinaiticus as their authorities and reject the massive amount of other evidences such as the church lectionaries. If 1 John 5:7-8 did not exist in the originals, then how could they have been quoted by the church fathers if it was non-existent.

Erasmus was a Greek scholar who was used of the Lord mightily as a precursor to the Reformation. He printed a Greek New Testament in 1516 and the Reformation took place in 1517. There is no such thing as a coincidence in the Kingdom of God, only a God-incident. Now Erasmus in reference to 1 John 5:7 originally did not want to include that portion unless a Greek manuscript could be found as evidence of its authenticity. He claimed that Greek manuscripts and even some Latin manuscripts did not have this verse in it. In due time Erasmus was presented with Codex Montfortianus which is in Dublin, Ireland and Codex Britannicus which both contained 1 John 5:7 and with this proof, he confidently placed these verses in his third edition of the Greek in 1522 and his last one in 1535. Erasmus died in 1536 but God had set the stage for the translation of the final true Bible in the English language which would be used of Christians until the Lord returned on the last day.

Some of the other evidences where 1 John 5:7-8 can be found are as follows:

Some Syriac Peshitto manuscripts, The Syriac Edition at Hamburg, Bishop Uscan's Armenian Bible, the Armenian Edition of John Zohrob, the first printed Georgian Bible.

The evidence is overwhelming for the authenticity of 1 John 5:7-8. Keep in mind that it was Origen who was the father of the false manuscripts who removed this verse as he did verses like Acts 8:37 and Luke 24:40. The Alexandrian school was no friend of the true manuscripts which were taken from Antioch and mutilated according to Gnostic beliefs

Affected Teachings

The mutilation of 1 John 5:7-8 in the Second Century was an attack upon the Trinity. The rejection of the Trinity is alive and well today in the Jehovah's Witnesses camp and is alive and well in the modern versions which agree totally with their New World Translation. Trinitarian theology is totally disbelieved by the Gnostics and many cult groups including the Jews. For any Theologian, Pastor, or Christian to endorse a version which attacks the Trinity, means they too disbelieve the Trinity or else they would not be defending the Gnostic view.

These verses are the most hotly contested by the modern version proponents simply because they disregard all the evidence that is available. This section of Scripture has been named the "Johannine Comma." 1 John 5:7-8 is as much a part of the original autographs as Jesus Himself was. Therefore, we can claim these verses as authentic without hesitation.

I would suggest that you print this information out and keep it as part of your library since 1 John 5:7-8 is a major bone of contention that the pro-modern version people tend to throw at us. If you have this information at hand, you will disarm them and cause them to go on the defensive and since most Christians are ignorant and refuse to do any research to combat their ignorance, you will have succeeded in proving your case and maybe winning over another Christian to the truth.

While the King James kept this into the translation, we should realize that it should not be taken for any doctrinal issue. For example, this passage should not be used in trying to explain the Trinity.

CHAPTER 20

ALLELUJAH IS NOT A WORD

Rev 19:1 Alleluia miss printed

The Greek Alphabet

This table gives the Greek letters, their names, equivalent English letters, and tips for pronouncing those letters which are pronounced differently from the equivalent English letters.

Α	α	alpha	a	"f**a**ther"
Β	β	beta	b	
Γ	γ	gamma	g	
Δ	δ	delta	d	
Ε	ϵ	epsilon	e	"**e**nd"
Ζ	ζ	zêta	z	
Η	η	êta	ê	"h**ey**"
Θ	θ	thêta	th	"**th**ick"
Ι	ι	iota	i	"**i**t"
Κ	κ	kappa	k	
Λ	λ	lamda	l	
Μ	μ	mu	m	
Ν	ν	nu	n	
Ξ	ξ	xi	ks	"bo**x**"
Ο	ο	omikron	o	"**o**ff"
Π	π	pi	p	
Ρ	ρ	rho	r	
Σ	σ, ς	sigma	s	"**s**ay"
Τ	τ	tau	t	
Υ	υ	upsilon	u	"p**u**t"
Φ	ϕ	phi	f	
Χ	χ	chi	ch	"B**ach**"
Ψ	ψ	psi	ps	
Ω	ω	omega	ô	"g**row**"

Breathings

The rough breathing is pronounced like an "h", and looks like a backwards comma written over a vowel. The smooth breathing is not pronounced at all, and looks like a regular comma written over a vowel. Note the difference between "en" and "hen":

smooth	rough
ἐν	ἕν
en	hen

There are two marks over the epsilon in "hen"; the first is the rough breathing, the second is the accent. When the Bible was penned the translators forgot, or made the mistake of not considering the (‘) which is an accent that produces an "h" sound. The original would thus read:

‘allelu(j)ah {keep in mind there are no j sounds as well}
The (‘) would equal an "h" sound thus making it hallelu(j)ah.

Therefore the Allelujah is a misprint in the book of Revelation. But wait! We have a bigger issue to tackle. How is it that we call Jesus, when there are no j sounds in Koine Greek?

I don't believe that God will be so critical for us pronouncing His name in error. The demons still know who you are talking about when you cast them out in that name. However, the correct name would be "YESHUA."

CHAPTER 21

SATAN CANNOT BE EVERYWHERE AT THE SAME TIME.

Eph 2:2 Satan is not everywhere at the same time

"In which you formerly walked according to the course of this world, according to the prince of the power of the air, of the spirit that is now working in the sons of disobedience."

Satan is not omnipresent (everywhere at the same time).

Satan is a fallen angel and what is true of angels is also true of Satan and his fallen angels, sometimes referred to as demons. Satan is not omnipresent (meaning present everywhere) - only God is omnipresent. Satan is a created being and can only be in one place at a time. He is not everywhere, but his followers, the fallen angels [demons] are and Satan can come to their aid. Satan is the head of a host of demons who are so numerous they make Satan's power and presence seem to be practically everywhere at once.

Satan is not omniscient (meaning all knowing). He is wise but not all wise. Satan has his vast army of demons that he obtains information from For example, Spiritualist, where we have people talking to the dead is not all false. Of course, no one can talk to the dead but Satan and his demons have worked to damn all mankind so they know about the dead and can communicate this information to the medium.

Satan is not omnipotent (all powerful). Omnipotent means all powerful and only God is all powerful. God would not be God unless He is all powerful. Satan is not all powerful but since mankind was created a little lower than the angels; Satan is much more powerful than mankind. Satan is subject to God as we see in the book of Job. Job 1:8-12.

Things to know about the enemy:

1. Satan wants us to believe that he doesn't really exist.
2. He wants people to have too high of a view of him, as if he were God. Just look at the movies and the power they portray evil having.
3. He can possess a non-believer. He can oppress a believer, i.e., give us a lot of trouble, but not possess a believer. Just think, there maybe people you know who are influenced by the devil or his demons.
4. The Devil can impose physical illness.
5. Satan tries to corrupt the true teaching of the gospel.

6. Satan, as an angelic being can: perform counterfeit miracles, produce mental illness, manipulate weather, keep believers in a state of depression, etc...

Ephesians6:11

". . . having put on the whole armor of God that ye may be able to stand against the wiles of the devil."

Satan is not all-powerful (omnipotent). God's armor can provide believers with a means of standing against him. We should put on the armor and keep it on, ". . . having put on the armor. . ."

CHAPTER 22

THREE KINDS OF FAITH

Mark 11:22 ...have FAITH in God.

Every time we see the word faith, we should not mistake it as being one word. There are three main views of faith as described in the Bible.

22And Jesus answered saying to them, "Have faith in God.

23"Truly I say to you, whoever says to this mountain, 'be taken up and cast into the sea, and does not doubt in his heart, but believes that what he says is going to happen, it will be granted him.

24"Therefore I say to you, all things for which you pray and ask, believe that you have received them, and they will be granted you.

25"Whenever you stand praying, forgive, if you have anything against anyone, so that your Father who is in heaven will also forgive you your transgressions.

26"But if you do not forgive, neither will your Father who is in heaven forgive your transgressions."

The Question is, what kind of faith is Jesus talking about?

The Bible speaks of three distinct kinds of faith.

The Grace of Faith

- This is saving faith which is given to all Christians (Acts 18:27; Philippians 1:29).
- All of us have this kind of faith
- Without it you and I are not saved.

The Fruit of Faith

- This is sanctifying faith which is developed only by those who are "filled by the Spirit" and thus "walk in the Spirit" (Galatians 5:16, 18, 22, 25).
- Some of us have this kind of faith
- Without it, we are not Spirit filled Christians.

The Gift of Faith

- This is a special faith rooted in a unique call of God to develop a distinct life message centered in proving God to the world by His meeting "impossible" needs (1 Corinthians 12:9).

- A few of us may have this kind of faith.
-

To each one of us is given a measure of faith. Saving faith or Grace of faith is necessary for salvation. But the faith described in Matthew 11 is the fruit of faith, which is to be developed as we walk this Christian way. Every day we should increase in our faith and confidence in God.

CHAPTER 23

DEATH IS UNNATURAL

John 11:33 death is a time of sorrow

The Death of Lazarus

Luke Chapter 16

11This He said, and after that He said to them, "Our friend Lazarus has fallen asleep; but I go, so that I may awaken him out of sleep."

13Now Jesus had spoken of his death, but they thought that He was speaking of literal sleep.

17So when Jesus came, He found that he had already been in the tomb four days.

21Martha then said to Jesus, "Lord, if you had been here, my brother would not have died.

22"Even now I know that whatever you ask of God, God will give you."

23Jesus said to her, "Your brother will rise again."

24Martha said to Him, "I know that he will rise again in the resurrection on the last day."

25Jesus said to her, "I am the resurrection and the life; he who believes in me will live even if he dies,

26and everyone who lives and believes in me will never die. Do you believe this?"

31Then the Jews who were with her in the house, and consoling her, when they saw that Mary got up quickly and went out, they followed her, supposing that she was going to the tomb to weep there.

32Therefore, when Mary came where Jesus was, she saw Him, and fell at His feet, saying to Him, "Lord, if you had been here, my brother would not have died."

33When Jesus therefore saw her weeping, and the Jews who came with her also weeping, He was deeply moved in spirit and was troubled,

34and said, "Where have you laid him?" They said to Him, "Lord, come and see."

35Jesus wept.

36So the Jews were saying, "See how He loved him!"

The Bible has ordained that each of us shall die once and then pass on to judgment (Hebrews 9:27). Death is the punishment placed on us because of Adam's sin and our sin (Genesis 2:16-17). This means that death is not unnatural or abnormal. It is unnatural and abnormal. Man was made to live and not die.

The World's view point of death
Death is natural
Death is a part of life
death should mean nothing to us
Death will always be here
The Christian view point of death
Death is unnatural
Death flows from sin
Death is a time of sorrow
Death will be done away with when Jesus returns

The Bible also speaks about another death, which is the death of our sinful nature. We are born in sin and shaped in iniquity. We have a sinful nature that we are constantly struggling against. There are three enemies against the Christian:

1. The Devil and his fallen angels.
2. The influence of this modern world and with all of its humanistic views.
3. Ourselves: Our own desire to do what we want to do against the will of God.

We need to fight this sinful nature through prayer and fasting. Only the Holy Spirit can give us the victory over our sinful self. Although this nature is alive, we are to treat it as if it were dead. So Paul tells us to reckon that it is dead. This is the struggle that the Apostle had (Romans chapter 7). We have to have this struggle with our sinful nature. Even though we will be tormented by our sinful flesh throughout this earthly life we need to treat it as if it were dead.

CHAPTER 24

SLAP ON THE CHEEK IS A PERSONAL INSULT

Whosoever smites thy right cheek, turn to him the other also (Matthew 5:39).

Jesus is well known for His continued emphasis on love, forgiveness, and "turning the other cheek." It is therefore surprising to find Jesus advising the disciples to buy a sword in Luke 22:36: "But now if you have a purse, take it, and also a bag; and if you don't have a sword, sell your cloak and buy one." Did Jesus in this verse advocate the use of a sword for self-defense purposes?

"TURN THE OTHER CHEEK" ALWAYS? It is true that Jesus said to turn the other cheek in Matthew 5:38-42. However, many scholars do not believe pacifism (or nonresistance) is the essential point of His teaching in this passage. These scholars do not believe

Jesus was teaching to "turn the other cheek" in virtually all circumstances. Even Christ did not literally turn the other cheek when smitten by a member of the Sanhedrin (see John 18:22-23).

The backdrop to this teaching is that the Jews considered it an insult to be hit in the face, much in the same way that we would interpret someone spitting in our face. Bible scholar R. C. Sproul comments: "What's interesting in the expression is that Jesus specifically mentions the right side of the face [Matthew 5:39]....If I hit you on your right cheek, the most normal way would be if I did it with the back of my right hand....To the best of our knowledge of the Hebrew language, that expression is a Jewish idiom that describes an insult, similar to the way challenges to duels in the days of King Arthur were made by a backhand slap to the right cheek of your opponent."

The principle taught in the Sermon on the Mount in Matthew 5:38-42 would thus seem to be that Christians should not retaliate when insulted or slandered (see also Romans 12:17-21). Such insults do not threaten a Christian's personal safety. The question of rendering insult for insult, however, is a far cry from defending oneself against a mugger or a rapist.

It is noteworthy that the Bible records many accounts of fighting and warfare. The providence of God in war is exemplified by His name YHWH ("The LORD of hosts"--Exodus 12:41). God is portrayed as the omnipotent Warrior-Leader of the Israelites. God, the LORD of hosts, raised up warriors among the Israelites called the shophetim (savior-deliverers). Samson, Deborah, Gideon, and others were anointed by the Spirit of God to conduct war. The New Testament commends Old Testament warriors for their military acts of faith (Hebrews 11:30-40). Moreover, it is significant that although given the opportunity to do so, none of the New Testament saints--nor even Jesus--are ever seen informing a military convert that he needed to resign from his line of work (Matthew 8:5-13; Luke 3:14).

Prior to His crucifixion, Jesus revealed to His disciples the future hostility they would face and encouraged them to sell their outer garments in order to buy a sword (Luke 22:36-38; cf. 2 Corinthians

11:26-27). Here the "sword" (Greek: maxairan) is a dagger or short sword that belonged to the Jewish traveler's equipment as protection against robbers and wild animals. A plain reading of the passage indicates that Jesus approved of self-defense.

Self-defense may actually result in one of the greatest examples of human love. Christ Himself said, "Greater love has no one than this, that he lay down his life for his friends" (John 15:14). When protecting one's family or neighbor, a Christian is unselfishly risking his or her life for the sake of others.

Theologians J. P. Moreland and Norman Geisler say that "to permit murder when one could have prevented it is morally wrong. To allow a rape when one could have hindered it is an evil. To watch an act of cruelty to children without trying to intervene is morally inexcusable. In brief, not resisting evil is an evil of omission, and an evil of omission can be just as evil as an evil of commission. Any man who refuses to protect his wife and children against a violent intruder fails them morally

In this passage Jesus commands His disciples to put a stop to all the retaliation. Again, rather than "eye for eye, tooth for tooth" retaliation, Jesus commanded: "Do not resist an evil person." To illustrate what He means, Jesus gives us four examples of what, in lieu of retaliation, our response should be. Each of these examples offers an alternative to vengeful anger. First: "If someone strikes you on the right cheek, turn to him the other also" (vs. 39). Many regard this verse (as Spurgeon points out) as "fanatical, utopian, and even cowardly."

Many stumble on this verse because they get hung up by extreme applications of it. They ask, "Does this mean Christians cannot be soldiers in war? Does this mean we cannot protect ourselves if a murderer invades our house? Etc..." In concentrating on these extremes, they are distracted from the heart of the matter: be first in peace; show love to your enemy. This is the principle Jesus is teaching. It is not a general rule that applies to any and every instance of evil perpetrated, locally and globally. It does not prevent Christians from serving in war, for war is a societal action, not a personal slap on the face. It does not prevent Christians from defending themselves from a murderer, for a murderer is not seeking to insult with a slap, but to take human life.

Having said this, let us get back to the heart of the matter: be first in peace; show love to your enemy. Let us review the situation: "If someone strikes you on the right cheek, turn to him the other also." A strike on the right cheek implies a slap with the back of the hand (since most people are right-handed). Such a slap is the action that accompanies a demeaning insult. In this situation, Jesus is commanding that, instead of rearing back with our right hand, we hold our peace, even "turn to him the other [cheek] also." Be first in peace. "But wait!" you may ask, "Would not turning the other cheek encourage more violence, more evil on his part?

In that way, would we not be inciting him to sin?" An interesting objection, but to turn the other cheek is the best option. Think about it. If you fight back, "eye for eye", you yourself are led into sin, and the perpetrator will think that his cruel action was justified. Alternatively, if you turn and run away from the insult, the perpetrator declares victory. His insult has achieved its objective. However, if you turn the other cheek, what has the perpetrator achieved? His insult has not achieved its desired effect, because you turn as if to want more. And then, what good would striking you again do for him, for you have literally asked for it? His failure to faze you, his failure at his insult, causes him to think twice about what he has done. It is then; his conscience begins its work, showing him the cruelty of his actions. By turning the other cheek, you follow Paul's exhortation: "Do not be overcome by evil, but overcome evil with good" (Rom. 12:21).

Our Lord Jesus, of course, practiced what He preached. He Himself was slapped in the face (see Matt. 26:67; John 19:3), and even more. Through all of His suffering, He had the power to retaliate, but chose not to. Instead, He chose to "overcome evil with good." In day-to-day life, we are seldom slapped in the face, but we are often insulted in other ways. Jesus' command to "turn the other cheek" can be applied perfectly to these day-to-day situations. Is there someone reviling you behind your back? Do not do the same behind his. In fact, in keeping with the spirit of "turning the other cheek", you would do well to admit your faults to him in person.

Does a coworker speak badly to your boss of your performance? Do not speak badly of his. "Turn the other cheek" and admit your faults to your boss. He may be impressed by your honesty. Are you often mocked to your face? "Turn the other cheek" and laugh right along. We will be challenged in this life. There are many different kinds of personalities we have to contend with. These people will try our nerves to see if we break. I like the way Robert M. Bramson, PhD., puts it in his book, "Coping with Difficult People." Dr. Bramson describes various types of hard to deal with people in several different categories:

- The Hostile Aggressive, who bullies by bombarding, making cutting remarks or throwing tantrums
- The Complainer, who gripes constantly but never attempts to solve the problem
- The Silent Unresponsive, who responds to all questions with just a yes or a no
- The Negativist, who responds to any situation as being undoable.
- The Know It All, who wants you to recognize that he or she knows everything about every subject.

It is hard to keep your sanity sometimes with these various personality types however, we need to try. Turning the other cheek means dealing with the non-sense without physical, mental or emotional retaliation. Only when the attack is posing a danger to you

or your family are we allowed to take attion. A preemptive strike may also be in order depending on the situation.

We need to endure personal insults when they come. As long as we are Christians we will be attacked. However, if we have the love of God in us we will tolerate the verbal abuse. Physical abuse is a different story. Read the early Church Fathers and their interpretation of Scripture. The Idea that a Christian cannot defend himself is anti-biblical. See the chapter on Pacifism.

CHAPTER 25

DRINKING WINE IS NOT A SIN

THE SIN IS TO BE DRUNK WITH WINE

St. John chapter 2.

Several verses encourage people to stay away from alcohol (Leviticus 10:9; Numbers 6:3; Deuteronomy 14:26; 29:6; 1 Samuel 1:15; Proverbs 20:1; 31:4, 6; Isaiah 5:11, 22; 24:9; 28:7; 29:9; 56:12; Micah 2:11; Luke 1:15). However, Scripture does not necessarily forbid a Christian from drinking beer, wine, or any other drink containing alcohol. Christians are commanded to avoid drunkenness (Ephesians 5:18). The Bible condemns drunkenness and its effects (Proverbs 23:29-35). Christians are also commanded to not allow their bodies to be "mastered" by anything (1 Corinthians 6:12; 2 Peter 2:19). Scripture also forbids a Christian from doing anything that might offend other Christians or might encourage them to sin against their conscience (1 Corinthians 8:9-13).

Jesus changed water into wine. It even seems that Jesus likely drank wine on occasion (John 2:1-11; Matthew 26:29). In New Testament times, the water was not very clean. Without modern sanitation efforts, the water was filled with bacteria, viruses, and all kinds of contaminants. Yet it doesn't negate the fact the He indeed drank it.

People in that time often drank wine (or grape juice) because it was far less likely to be contaminated. In 1 Timothy 5:23, Paul was instructing Timothy to stop drinking the water (which was probably causing his stomach problems) and instead drink wine. The Greek word for wine in the Bible is the most basic everyday word for wine. In that day, wine was fermented, but not to the degree it is today. It is incorrect to say that it was grape juice, but it is also incorrect to say that it was the same thing as the wine we use today. Again, Scripture does not necessarily forbid Christians from drinking beer, wine, or any other drink containing alcohol.

Alcohol is not, in and of itself, tainted by sin. It is, rather, drunkenness and addiction to alcohol that a Christian must absolutely refrain from (Ephesians 5:18; 1 Corinthians 6:12). There are principles in the Bible, however, that make it extremely difficult to argue that a Christian drinking alcohol in any quantity is pleasing to God. The commemorative wine of the Last Supper Passover Memorial was alcohol not grape juice. The word "WINE" in the New Testament is the Greek word "OINOS", which itself comes from the Hebrew word "YAHYIN". Yahyin means "to effervesce, be fermented" (Strong's ref. # 3631, 3196). It is this alcohol wine which Paul advises Christians to use in small amounts "for thy stomach's sake" (I Tim. 5:23). "But", some say, "Jesus mentions 'fruit of the vine', and my preacher says that this means only grape juice". Not true!

"Fruit of the vine" can be understood to mean either wine OR grape juice. So how do we know which one the Passover Wine was? For starters, those who teach that it is unbiblical to ever drink any alcohol wine are off base Scripturally simply from the above original text meanings of the word "wine". The Bible definitely tells us that Yahweh's faithful people certainly did partake of fermented wine, and that in moderation, it is actually a health benefit.

It must be understood that grape juice remains unfermented only one day. After day one fermentation begins and froth begins to form on the top. Since there was no method of refrigeration in Bible days, and the Passover was six months AFTER the fall grape harvest, any juice in Palestine would have long since fermented into full wine by the time of the Spring Passover. Secular history tells us that the Judeans and Greeks considered the phrase "fruit of the vine" to be an idiom applied to alcohol wine used for ceremonial offerings. (Westminster Dictionary of the Bible, 1944 ed., page 641). Since we're more interested in a Scriptural rather than the historical analysis (even though it does lend a hand in our search), what was the connotation that Jesus Himself gave to the term "fruit of the vine"?

At the Last Supper Jesus said, "I will not drink henceforth of this fruit of the vine UNTIL that day when I drink it anew with you in my Father's Kingdom". (Mat.26:29) What did He mean by this? Jesus is presently in the Heavenly Temple serving as our High Priest. (Heb.4:14) Biblically, the High Priest was instructed, "Do not drink wine (fermented Yahyin) or strong drink (shawthaw - stronger liquor) ... when ye go into the Tabernacle." (Lev.10:8-11) The Old Testament High Priest was a type of Christ. His position symbolized events yet to be fulfilled. Christ was referring to His own Priestly duties when He told those in His company that He would refrain from drinking the "fruit of the vine" until he returned as King. If he were drinking only grape juice at the Last Supper there would be no reason for Jesus to even mention His curious "drink prohibition" since grape juice itself can be consumed in any place or at any time. We know from this account that the Passover wine Jesus was drinking with the Apostles WAS INDEED ALCOHOL WINE which the High Priest could not use in the Tabernacle of Yahweh.

Additionally, wine and not grape juice IS the symbol used to represent Christ's blood shed in the streets of Jerusalem and on the Cross. The Old Testament taught that real wine depicted the Messiah's blood that would be shed. Although animal sacrifices likewise depicted the Messiah's yet to come shed blood, that symbolism was also reinforced by the ceremonial drink offerings of fermented wine (yahyin) as we see in Numbers 15:10 and 28:14. Such drink offerings represented blood. (see Psalm 16:4) Christ "poured out (offered) His soul (life) unto death." (Is. 53:12), since "the life of the flesh is in the blood." (Lev. 17:11) Thus, according to the Bible it was "Yahyin", alcohol wine, which represented the blood of Messiah. Alcohol wine has a "zing" to the taste and livens/awakens the mouth. It's also a token of bodily properties that don't decay (wine keeps it's body even as it ages) reminding us of perpetuity.

Grape juice to the taste is comparatively flat, not lively as a good wine and it attracts flies when spilled, depicting a mortal blood that attracts Beelzebub, lord of dung and death. (Mat.12:24). What about the term "new wine"? Some claim that this merely means grape juice, but this claim does not stand Bible scrutiny. On the contrary, new wine usually means regular alcohol wine in the Bible as new wine can cause drunkenness (Joel 1:5), and can take away understanding (Hosea 4:11). The disciples were accused of being drunk with new wine on Pentecost. (Acts 2:13, 15). This is not a property of grape juice. The conclusion that new wine refers specifically to grape juice is not supported by Scriptures.

From the very first clue related to a "bread and wine" ceremony, the Scriptures teach this to be a fermented drink. The King of Salem, Melchizedek, (possibly Christ in another form), brought bread and wine (yahyin) to Abram and blessed him (Gen. 14:18, 19). This "cup" recognized a type of fury and was brought to Abram just after Abram slaughtered the kings of Sodom in battle. As long as there is war with evil forces in the world, this particular "cup of spilled blood" shall be drunk by both evil doers and God's faithful participating in the battle.

Drinking from the fermented cup (yahyin) of wine has the ability to cause fury (Jer.25:15), madness (Jer. 51:7), astonishment (Ps. 60:3), and violence (Pr. 4:17). Grape juice has no such ability. Most important to realize is that all of these things were poured out upon Jesus at His crucifixion. Although innocent, He did "drink of this cup" of horrible suffering (Mat.26:39). Christ then said that His followers would likewise "drink of His cup" (Mat.20:23) meaning that the world will persecute His faithful in many different ways.

When we drink of the wine at "Communion Service" we are attesting to the above mentioned "fury, madness, astonishment, and violence" which Christ endured at the crucifixion. Grape juice could never symbolize this suffering as does wine. Unintentionally, grape juice partakers at the Communion Bread and Wine Ceremony are denying Christ's cup of suffering according to how the Bible defines the attributes of fermented wine.

The partaking of alcohol wine also means that a Christian knows he has entered into a life of suffering for the testimony of the Cross. The potentially dangerous "wine" of tribulation, persecution, and martyrdom follows the true Church [Ecclesia] (see Acts 12:2; Rev.1:19; 17:6). So also does a life of self sacrifice (Rom.12:1; I Pet.2:21). "All that will live Godly in Christ Jesus shall suffer persecution." (II Tim. 3:12) "We must through much tribulation enter the Kingdom of God." (Acts 14:22).

Drinking wine should not be a subject that we divide over. This will remain an issue that some will struggle with probably throughout their Christian lives. “If meat offends your brother, don’t eat it.” It would be wrong for someone to consume this in front of someone who would be weak or tempted by this. Common sense would tell you that you should not go to the bar if you are struggling with this issue. Remember, whether you like it or not it is being drunk that is the sin, not drinking.

1. "Wine" is mentioned 260 times in the Bible and "strong drink" is mentioned 21 times. In the Hebrew and in the Greek,

"wine" refers to fermented grape juice and "strong drink" refers to the alcohol fermented from fruits and grains, and is called "beer" or "hard liquor" today.

2. The drinking of alcohol was universal except for certain priests. Abraham and Melchizedek (Gen. 14:18), Isaac (Gen. 27:25), Jacob (Gen. 27:28), Boaz (Ruth 3:7), a Levite (Jud. 19:19), Paul and Timothy (I Tim. 5:23), and even Jesus (Lk. 7:33-34) drank wine.

3. Both wine and strong drink were used in the worship of God (Gen. 14:28; Exo. 29:39-40; Deut. 14:26; Num. 28:7). If they were "the devil's brew" or "demon rum," God would have never commanded them to be part of worship.

4. They are viewed as the blessing of God in the Bible (Gen. 27:28; Psa. 104:15; Pro. 3:9-10; Isa. 55:1-2; Ecc. 10:19; Zech. 10:7).

5. Jesus not only drank wine but He even made it for others (John 2:1-11 cf. 4:46).

6. A little wine with your meal is viewed as good for your health (I Tim. 5:23).

7. Both strong drink and wine were used for mental health (Pro. 31:6-7).

8. The wise woman prepares wine for a meal (Pro. 9:1-5).

CHAPTER 26

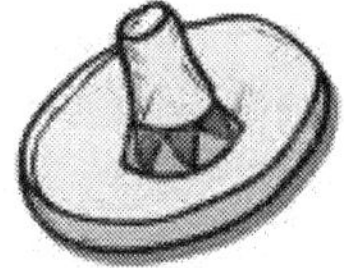

WE DON'T NEED TO WEAR HEAD COVERINGS

1 Corinthians chapter 11

It is our desire to give a practical exposition of one of the most difficult portions of the New Testament. It has been many years since any significant evangelical labor has been expended on the head-covering issue. Since this practice is largely confined to Catholic or Anabaptist denominations, most evangelicals have never thought through their own position on the subject. In years past, there has been very little interaction between Anabaptist groups and evangelical churches. But this is changing. Due to several popular family-life seminars, evangelicals and Anabaptists find themselves sitting together. This has led to a natural curiosity on the part of both groups. Evangelicals ask, "Why do your women wear those little caps?" and the Anabaptists ask, "Why don't your women wear head coverings?"

It is in this context of mutual love and respect that we now put forth why evangelical women are not required to wear a head covering. We do this to fulfill the royal mandate found in I Peter 3:15, "Be prepared to give a reasonable reply to those who ask you about the hope you harbor in your heart, but do so with humility and respect."

This study is not intended to be an attack on any group, but rather a practical exposition of the evangelical position on head coverings.

The Context

In terms of the immediate context, before Paul takes up the subject of head coverings, he lays before the Corinthians his heart's desire that they should follow his example by conforming themselves to the customs of the ethnic group in whose community they live. Perhaps a paraphrase of I Corinthians 10:32-11:1 would help to bring out Paul's introduction to his discussion on head coverings:

"Do not create unnecessary stumbling blocks or hindrances (to the free preaching of the Gospel) among Jews, Greeks or even Christians. I conform myself to the social customs of whatever ethnic or national group that I am seeking to evangelize. I do this because I am not selfish. I can reach more people for Christ by my adopting their customs than by my hanging on to my cultural background. So then, you should follow my example in conforming yourselves to the customs of the society in which you live. Remember, even Christ adopted our customs in order to avoid any unnecessary hindrances. Follow me as I follow Christ."

From the context, it is clear that Paul's concern as he approached the issue of head coverings was that of social conformity to cultural customs for the sake of the Gospel. In I Corinthians 10:32-11:1, the divine principle of rule is set forth. Then in I Corinthians 11:2-16, Paul applies this principle to the Corinthians in the light of their non-compliance with this very basic principle of the Christian life. Having stated this principle which he is going to apply, Paul wisely begins by praising them before he chides them. We will paraphrase here and elsewhere to bring out the force of the original. "I would like to thank you for remembering me personally and for holding firm to the things which I taught you" (v.2). After his brief "thank you," Paul sets forth a basic theological concept which would provide the common ground between them. Thus, he first begins with what they all agree upon and then he proceeds to the area of disagreement.

Now, one of the things I taught you is that Christ is the 'head' of every man, the husband is the 'head' of his wife and God (the Father) is the 'head' of Christ." Although Christ as God the Son is not in any way inferior to God the Father in terms of being, essence, glory, nature or person yet, for the purposes of executing the plan of salvation, there is a voluntary subordination of the Son to the Father. God the Son as "Christ" i.e., the Messiah, the Servant of the Lord, looked to the Father for all things.

In the same way, although women are not inferior to men in any way, for the purposes of marriage harmony, God has ordained that the husband shall be the "head" of the wife. Just as there is a voluntary functional subordination of Christ to the Father, so there is a voluntary functional subordination of the wife to the husband. A problem in the Corinthian church had arisen because the women had misunderstood Paul's teaching that "in Christ" there is neither male nor female" (Gal. 3:28). Paul did teach that women were not inferior to men; but he was speaking in terms of their nature and person. He was not denying a functional subordination which was pragmatically necessary to maintain marriage harmony. Thus he skillfully shows that just as both equality and subordination exist in the divine family of the Trinity, both things can and should exist in the human family as well. It is not either equality or subordination but both equality and subordination.

Paul's position is a third way which escapes the women's liberation position and the chauvinistic sexist positions at the same time. Having clarified his position on equality and subordination in the Divine and human family, Paul now applies the principle of cultural adaptation for the sake of the Gospel in vs.4-6. There are several exegetical observations which should be pointed out.

Paul is clearly referring to the attire of men and woman when they are personally engaged in taking part in public worship. He envisions both the man and the woman as publicly praying or prophesying. This is so clear that nearly all commentators agree. This concept leads us to several observations. There is nothing in the text to indicate what a man or woman is to wear outside of the public assembly.

To state that a woman should wear a covering at all times means that no man can wear a covering at any time. Since some of the Anabaptists have their women wear caps at all times, they are not consistent, for their men wear hats much of the time. Any deviation from verse four makes any obedience to verse five hypocritical and selective. To gloss over verse four and to dogmatize on verse five reveals faulty exegesis as well as sexist application.

It must also be pointed out that since the early church thought of itself as a Body and not a building, it was not entering a "church" building that required the presence or absence of a head-covering. Paul limits his discussion to those who are "up front," i.e., those who are actually taking an active and public role in praying or prophesying. First, any putting off or on of a head covering merely because one enters a building reveals a faulty concept of the Biblical doctrine of the church. To be consistent, the only time you could observe this rule on head coverings is when the people of God meet in small groups or in the assembly and when you are standing up to pray or prophesy publicly before others.

Second, where did the custom of head coverings being put off or on when engaged in public praying or prophesying originate? What are the origins of this practice? The issue as discussed by Paul assumed that the Corinthians knew of the practice. Their problem was non-compliance and not ignorance. Paul referred to a bald head as "public disgrace." What "public" did he have in mind? Who thought that men with a head covering and women without a head covering when engaged in public praying or prophesying were disgraceful or disrespectful? Did it come from the Bible of their day, the Old Testament? Is there, in the Old Testament, any examples, commands or precepts that it is wrong for a man to pray or prophesy with his head covered or for a woman to do so without her head covered? NO! Indeed, the High Priest, on the most holy day, covered his head with a miter in order to go into the Holy of Holies before the presence of God! There is no Old Testament practice to which Paul would possibly be referring. The practice did not originate in God's Word. This leads us to the following conclusions—the head covering practice was not a Scriptural issue or problem. Paul never once quoted the O.T. or said, "It is written" in reference to the practice of head coverings. There is no O.T. laws to which Paul could appeal. The practice of head coverings cannot be a Moral Law, for all Moral Laws were revealed in the Scriptures, and the Jews were forbidden to look elsewhere for any more. The head covering practice was not a part of the essence of worship. If it were, it would have been revealed in the O.T.

Thus, while the functional subordination of women was taught in the O.T., the practice of head coverings was not needed to illustrate or support it. Thus, the practice of head coverings is not essential to the concept of subordination. Second, did it come from Jewish culture? Did the Jews of Paul's day observe the custom he described to the Corinthians? Answer: NO! According to overwhelming evidence, the Jews practiced exactly the opposite. Jewish men wore a covering, and the women went without a covering.

Dr. J. B. Lightfoot comments,

"It was the custom of the Jews that they prayed not, unless first their heads were veiled and that for this reason-that by this rite they might show themselves reverent and ashamed before God and unworthy with an open face to behold Him."

Even T. Edwards admits, "Among the Jews the men veiled their faces in prayer. The Tallith dates back to the time of Christ and probably earlier" (Handbook to the Bible, p. 194.

"An unveiled woman, therefore, in Corinth proclaimed herself as not only insubordinate, but as immodest. If she wishes to be regarded as a reputable woman, let her conform to the established usage. But if she has no regard to her reputation, let her act as other women of her class. She must conform either to the reputable or disreputable class of her sex, for a departure from the one is conforming to the other. These imperatives are not to be taken as commands, but rather as expressing what consistence would require."

The Expositor's Greek Testament, vol. II, pp. 872-875:

"Amongst the Greeks only the (prostitutes), so numerous in Corinth, went about unveiled; slave-women wore the shaven head-also a punishment of the adulterous: with these the Christian woman who emancipates herself from becoming restraints of dress, is in effect identified."

A.T. Robertson, Word Pictures in the New Testament, vol. IV, pp. 159-160: "Probably some of the women had violated this custom. Among Greeks only the hetairai, so numerous in Corinth, went about unveiled; slave-women wore the shaven head." "He does not here condemn the act, but the breach of custom which would bring reproach. A woman convicted of adultery had her hair shaven (Isaiah 7:20). The Justinian Code prescribed shaving the head for an adulterous woman whom the husband refused to receive back after two years. Paul does not tell Corinthian Christian women to put themselves on a level with courtesans."

"Paul means that a woman praying or prophesying uncovered puts herself in public opinion on a level with a courtesan." What did these head coverings look like? Charles Hodge comments, "The veils worn by Grecian women were of different kinds. One and perhaps the most common, was the peplum or mantle, which in public was thrown over the head and enveloped the whole person. The other was more in the fashion of the common eastern veil which covered the face, with the exception of the eyes. In one form or other, the custom was universal for all respectable women to appear veiled in public.

The apostle therefore says, that a woman who speaks in public with her head uncovered, dishonored her head. Here (it) is used, her own head; not her husband, but herself. This is plain, not only from the force of the words, but from the next clause, for that is even all one as if she were shaven. This is the reason why she disgraces herself. She puts herself in the same class with women whose hair has been cut off. Cutting off the hair, which is the principal natural ornament of women, was either a sign of grief, Deut. 21:12 or a disgraceful punishment. The literal translation of this clause is: she is one and the same thing with one who is shaven. She assumes the characteristic mark of a disreputable woman."

In order to show that the Greek customs were acceptable to Christians and not in conflict with Christian thought, Paul argues: (vs.7-15). A man can have his head uncovered; is not he created in the image and glory of God? But, a woman was created in the (image) and glory of man. So, she can be covered. Remember that Eve was created out of Adam and not Adam out of Eve. Adam was not created to be Eve's help-meet, but Eve was created to be his help-meet. For this reason and because of the angels, a woman can have a head-covering, which (in Corinth) is a sign of being under authority.

This is not to say that men are independent of (or better than) women or that women are independent of (or better than) men. All men are born from women just as Eve came from Adam. Everything in the end comes from God. So, you decide what is proper with your own sense of propriety: Is it proper (in Corinth) for a woman to pray publicly to God with her head uncovered? Does not (Greek and Corinthian) custom and culture tell you that long hair on a man is shameful while on a woman, it is her glory? For long hair is given to her as a covering. Now, if anyone really wants to fight about this, let him or her know that we and the other churches do not allow the practice of women publicly praying or prophesying with an uncovered head.

Does Paul ever argue for moral laws or absolute truths by appealing to people to examine their feelings? NO! This insight strengthens the evangelical position. Paul is dealing with an application of a general principle. The application is culturally bound and limited. The principle will be applied according to each culture. That this is what Paul is saying in verse 13 is supported by nearly all classic commentaries.

"Paul appeals to the sense of propriety among the Christians." In verse 13, Paul is pointing to a subjective witness in the Corinthians themselves. First of all their own sense of propriety, shaped by the customs of the culture in which they lived, spoke out in favor of Paul's argument. Secondly while engaged in public worship, men should not have their heads covered. Neither should women have their heads uncovered while leading in prayer or publicly prophesying. Thirdly, the cultural upbringing of the Corinthians was a valid witness for Paul's case. Fourthly, having appealed to a subjective witness within the Corinthians, Paul now appeals to an objective witness in v. 14. He appeals to "nature" as "teaching" them that while it is shameful for men to have long hair, it is the woman's glory to have long hair. What Paul meant by "nature" is a much debated subject. There are as many opinions as there are commentators. Even though a "final" interpretation is perhaps impossible (cf. II Pet. 3:16), several things are abundantly clear.

(1) Since Paul has just appealed to a subjective witness in verse 13, he is surely not appealing to something subjective again. Whatever he means by "nature," it refers to something external or objective to the Corinthians. (2) This objective witness cannot be

based on a Newtonian world view in which there are "natural laws" inherent in the creation. Many commentators have made the fatal mistake of reading 19th and 20th Century scientific world views into this First Century text. Thus Paul could not mean "natural law" when he wrote "nature." Any interpretation which claims that Paul is talking about "laws in the creation order" is eisegesis and not exegesis. (3) Since the Greek word translated "nature" is used in various ways in the New Testament, nothing can be "proved" by its etymology. The safest meaning of the word "nature" would be the objective cultural customs of the society in which they lived. This would be the normal everyday meaning of "nature" in any given culture.

As Matthew Henry pointed out, "custom is in a great measure the rule of decency." 7 Every culture legislates what is "natural" and "unnatural," i.e., what is against "nature" or in conformity to "nature." "The instinctive consciousness of propriety on this point had been established by custom and had become nature."

Conclusion

To those who wish to observe the rule on head-covering, we say "May God richly bless you." But let them not fall into the assumption that their worship is acceptable because of a hat, cap or scarf. Let them not judge others who do not follow the rule. Let them place the emphasis on the inner and spiritual attitudes and Christ-like character qualities which make a believer's worship acceptable to God. Let them not think that they are more "holy" because of the clothing they wear. According to the New Covenant, our holiness is to be seen in our character-not in distinctive clothing.

To those who do not feel that the rule on head-coverings applies to them, we say, "May God richly bless you." But let them not judge those who practice head coverings. Let them not get proud over their "liberty." Let them not scorn the weaker brothers and sisters whose conscience tells them to observe the rule. In the light of Rom. 14:1-23, let us allow the love of God to temper our passions and the truth of God to guide our convictions. There is no reason why Christians who

disagree over this non-essential aspect of public worship cannot dwell together in unity. This was only a custom. If Churches wish to practice this, no one should object. However, the problem will come if people try to make this passage Law. It was a custom in which God chose to separate His people from the heathen.

CHAPTER 27

PETER IS NOT THE ROCK

Upon this rock I will build my Church,

Matthew chapter 16

KING JAMES VERSION

And I say also to thee, That thou art Peter (Petros), and upon this rock (Petra) I will build my church; and the gates of hell shall not prevail against it. Matthew 16.18

This single verse of Scripture is the foundation upon which is laid all of Rome's claims to papal primacy, pre-eminence, infallibility, jurisdiction, etc. In fact, the very existence of the papacy, as distinct from every other bishopric in the Church, stands or falls upon the validity, or the invalidity, of Rome's interpretation of this verse of Scripture. According to Rome's interpretation, Peter (gr. petros) and the 'rock' (gr. petra) are one and the same. This, in spite of the fact that the two words carry different meanings.

"In secular Greek pétra denotes a large 'rock,' but also a 'cliff'; or 'rocky mountain chain.' Figuratively it suggests firmness, immovability, and hardness. pétros is more often used for smaller rocks, stones, or pebbles."

Theological Dictionary of the New Testament, by Geoffrey W. Bromily.

Rome says that the reason Peter is called petros is because petros is the masculine form of the feminine noun petra (meaning 'rock'), and it was fitting that Peter's name should be masculine. However, I have never seen them offer an explanation for why the feminine petra is always used in the Scriptures to refer to Christ, but never the masculine petros, which is only used to refer to Peter. I believe it is because, by definition, petra more accurately typifies Christ, while petros more accurately typifies Peter. It is upon the petra that Christ is building his Church.

But Rome claims that, on the basis of this verse of Scripture, Peter is the 'rock' on which Christ is building his Church, and that the honor accorded to Peter alone is the rightful heritage of the bishops of Rome whom, they claim, are the successors of Peter and the 'vicars' of Christ. Further, they claim that, therefore, the bishops of Rome are endowed with primacy over all other bishops, infallibility in doctrines of faith and morals, and supremacy and jurisdiction over all the members of Christ's Body, the Church. See Matthew 16.18 for some examples from Vatican I & II of these claims.

In taking this position, Rome ignores the fact that Peter tells us that Christ is the Rock on which we are being built upon:

If indeed ye have tasted that the Lord is gracious.

To whom coming, as to a living stone, rejected indeed by men, but chosen by God, and precious,

Ye also, as living stones, are built up a spiritual house, an holy priesthood, to offer up spiritual sacrifices, acceptable to God by Jesus Christ.

Therefore also it is contained in the scripture, Behold, I lay in Zion a chief corner stone, elect, precious: and he that believeth on him shall not be confounded.

To you therefore who believe he is precious: but to them who are disobedient, the stone which the builders rejected, the same is made the head of the corner,

And a stone of stumbling, and a rock [Petra] of offence, even to them who stumble at the word, being disobedient: to this also they were appointed. (I Peter 2.3-8).

In I Peter 2.6 and Ephesians 2.20, Christ is called the Chief Cornerstone of the foundation. The Greek word here is akrogoniaios, or the 'extreme corner'. Rome claims that this means the 'capstone', which could be a possible translation of the word in another context—but not in this context. Holding this view enables them to continue to maintain the view that Peter is the foundation 'rock' upon which the Church is built upon. But that is not an honest interpretation of this passage of Scripture. Thus it is clear that Christ, and not Peter, is the Chief Cornerstone of the foundation, and the Rock, on which the Church is being built.

Paul writes in Ephesians 2.20 that Christ is the Chief Corner of the foundation:

And are built upon the foundation of the apostles and prophets, Jesus Christ himself being the chief corner stone;

And Paul writes in 1 Corinthians 3.10-11 that Christ is the foundation upon which we must build:

According to the grace of God which is given to me, as a wise master builder, I have laid the foundation, and another build upon it. But let every man take heed how he buildeth upon it.

For other foundation can no man lay than that which is laid, which is Jesus Christ.

And then there are the popish apologists and Greek exegetes, like this one, who says:

Apart from translations others try to say that when Jesus said "and on THIS rock I will build My Church" he was actually referring to himself. This is another big mistake, when a demonstrative pronoun is used with the Greek word for "and", which is "kai", the pronoun refers back to the preceding noun. In other words, when Jesus Says, "You are rock, and on THIS rock I will build My Church", the second rock He refers to HAS to be the SAME rock and the first one. Peter is the Rock in BOTH cases.

This is what could be called bad Greek. It is not any rule of Greek grammar; and it does not offer any explanation why the sentence goes from second person masculine to third person feminine, if both nouns refer to Peter. The switch to the third person, while still speaking to Peter, seems to indicate that the rock is something other than Peter.

How strong are the delusions of papal idolatry that cause people to willingly invent such reasonings, and others to blindly place their faith and trust and confidence in them? But, Christ said that the blind follow their blind leaders into the ditch.

The feminine demonstrative pronoun taute is used 31 times in the New Testament (including Matthew 16.18). Five of these times it is in close proximity following kai. In none of these five instances (including Matthew 16.18) does it refer back to a precedent noun. Taute, in these instances, always and only refers to the noun which it modifies, which in the case of Matthew 16.18 is "rock.

While there may be instances where a demonstrative pronoun can refer back to a precedent noun (e.g. Matthew 21.23), it surely is not a grammatical rule in Greek that it must—nor even that it most often does.

A more capable examination of this passage can be found in the treatise The Rock of the Apostle Peter, by Panagiotis Boumis (Translated by David Turner), wherein it is shown that the passage can properly be interpreted as Christ being the Rock on which the Church is built—and that there is reason for so interpreting it.

At first, we cannot exclude the interpretation that the "Πετρα" named by the Lord is the confession about Christ ως Υιον του Θεου του ζωντως, or rather Jesus Christ Himself. This very formulation of the passage allows for just such an interpretation. The passage, as is known, runs, Καγω δε σοι λεγω οτι συ ει Πετρος, και επι ταυτη τη πετρα οικοδομησο μου την εκκλησιαν, and not συ ει Πετρος και επι σε οικοδομησο μου την εκκλησιαν. Thus we can say that this change in the term (Πετρος - Πετρα) in the two sentences, in conjunction with the existence of the preceding confession Συ ει ο Χριστος, ο υιος του Θεου του ζωντως not only provides us with a possibility but also a reason to render this passage in the above mentioned interpretation.

The writer goes on to explain that it is also not impossible to understand Peter as being the rock—but not to the exclusion of the other apostles, who all are rocks in the foundation of the Church (e.g. Ephesians 2.20; Revelation 21.14). He concludes his discussion like this:

In retrospect, one may say that the clearest interpretation of και επι ταυτη τη πετρα οικοδομησο μου την εκκλησιαν is the following: I will build my Church also on this rock, in which you confessed, that Jesus Christ, as upon solid ground and on you, Peter, as confessing in Him and constituting thus a foundation stone on this ground, without excluding but rather understanding that I will also build on other foundation stones, namely the rest of the Apostles, who will proclaim the same truth in Christ upon whom will rest the teachings of the Church concerning me.

There is nothing in the New Testament that gives any support to the thought that Peter was given any place of pre-eminence above the other apostles in the Church, or that he is the 'rock' upon which the Church is being built. Peter, James, and John were at times present with Christ apart from the others: the Transfiguration, the healing of Jairus's daughter, Gethsemane; and, at times, Peter acted as a leader among the disciples. But it is a far stretch from that to claim that Peter is the rock on which Christ builds his Church—especially when the weightier evidence indicates that Christ Himself is that Rock. Peter, in humility, would rather have had the attitude of John the Baptist who said of Christ, "He must increase, but I must decrease" (John 3:30). Rome has rather ever and always sought to increase itself to the disparagement of Christ and the rest of the Church.

CHAPTER 28

GOD IS NOT THE EVIL DOER

I will harden Pharaohs heart, Exodus 4:21.

"And the LORD said unto Moses, When thou goest to return into Egypt, see that thou do all those wonders before Pharaoh, which I have put in thine hand: but I will harden his heart, that he shall not let the people go."

As we look at this subject of God and evil, let us start off by stating that God made everything, but He allowed evil to manifest. This doesn't make God directly responsible for sin and evil, this just means that sin and evil came out of what God had made. God created Pharaoh, and Pharaoh became greedy and evil. God hardening Pharaoh's heart was God simply doing to Pharaoh what Pharaoh had already done to himself. God just let him go. If God were to let us all go, we would all do evil beyond our imagination. It is the Holy Spirit that grieves within us and helps us to try and do the right thing.

The heart of man is wicked. If left to our own devices we would do all sorts of evil. God let Pharaoh go! This is what is known in theology as the cause of secondary agency. God is not directly responsible but he allowed the act to take place. So through the process of secondary agency, Pharaoh did what was in his heart to do and God let him. Man wants to do evil; it is in our nature to do so. If we had a choice we would choose evil over good. God's sovereignty in the matter of evil usually does not have a God-entranced world view. For them, now God is sovereign, and now he is not. Now he is in control, and now he is not. Now he is good and reliable when things are going well, and when they go bad, well, maybe he's not. Now he's the supreme authority of the universe, and now he is in the dock with human prosecutors peppering him with demands that he give an account of himself.

We need to settle in our minds biblically, intellectually and emotionally, that God has ultimate control of all things, including evil, and that this is gracious and precious beyond words, then a marvelous stability and depth come into that person's life and they develop a "God-entranced world view." When a person believes, with the Heidelberg Catechism (Question 27), that "The almighty and everywhere present power of God . . . upholds heaven and earth, with all creatures, and so governs them that herbs and grass, rain and drought, fruitful and barren years, meat and drink, health and sickness, riches and poverty, yea, all things, come not by chance, but by his fatherly hand" – when a person believes and cherishes that truth, they have the key to a God-entranced world view. God has absolute sovereign control over all things, including evil, because it is Biblical.

Evidence of God's Control

First, then, consider the evidence that God controls all things, including evil. When I speak of evil, I have two kinds in mind, natural and moral. Natural evil we usually refer to as calamities: hurricanes, floods, disease, and all the natural ways that death and misery strike without human cause. Moral evil we usually refer to as sin: murder, lying, adultery, stealing, all the ways that people fail to love each other. So what we are considering here is that God rules the world in such a way that all calamities and all sin remain in His ultimate control and therefore within His ultimate design and purpose.

The denial of God's foreknowledge of human and demonic choices is a buttress to the view that God is not in control of evils in the world and therefore has no purpose in them. God's uncertainty about what humans and demons are going to choose strengthens the case that he does not plan those choices and therefore does not control them or have particular purposes in them.

For example, Gregory Boyd, in his book God at War, says, "Divine goodness does not completely control or in any sense will evil." Jesus nor his disciples seemed to understand God's absolute power as absolute control. They prayed for God's will to be done on earth, but this assumes that they understand that God's will was not yet being done on earth (Mt. 6:10). Hence neither Jesus nor his disciples assumed that there had to be a divine purpose behind all events in history. Rather, they understood the cosmos to be populated by a myriad of free agents, some human, some angelic, and many of them evil. The manner in which events unfold in history was understood to be as much a factor of what these agents individually and collectively will as it was a matter of what God himself willed.

In other words "the Bible does not assume that every particular evil has particular godly purpose behind it." This is diametrically opposed to what I believe the Bible teaches and what this message is meant to commend to you for your earnest consideration.

Life and death

The Bible treats human life as something God has absolute rights over. He gives it and takes it according to his will. We do not own it or have any absolute rights to it. It is a trust for as long as the owner wills for us to have it. To have life is a gift and to lose it is never an injustice from God, whether he takes it at age five or age ninety-five.

When Job lost his ten children at the instigation of Satan, he would not give Satan the ultimate causality. He said, "Naked I came from my mother's womb, and naked I shall return there. The LORD gave and the LORD has taken away. Blessed be the name of the LORD" (Job 1:21). And, lest we think Job was mistaken, the author adds, "In all this Job did not sin or charge God with wrong" (Job 1:22 RSV).

In Deuteronomy 32:39 God says, "There is no god besides Me; it is I who put to death and give life. I have wounded and it is I who heal, and there is no one who can deliver from my hand." When David made Bathsheba pregnant, the Lord rebuked him by taking the child. 2 Samuel 12:15 says, "Then the LORD struck the child that Uriah's widow bore to David, so that he was sick . . . . Then it happened on the seventh day that the child died." Life belongs to God. He owes it to no one. He may give it and take it according to his infinite wisdom. James says "You do not know what your life will be like tomorrow. You are a vapor that appears for a little while and then vanishes away. . . . You ought to say, 'If the Lord wills, we will live and also do this or that'" (James 4:14-15; see 1 Samuel 2:6-7).

Disease

One of the calamities that threaten life is disease. In Exodus 4:11, God says to Moses, when he was fearful about speaking, "Who has made man's mouth? Who makes him dumb, or deaf, or seeing, or blind? Is it not I, the LORD?" In other words, behind all disease and disability is the ultimate will of God. Not that Satan is not involved; he is probably always involved one way or the other with destructive purposes (Acts 10:38). But his power is not decisive. He cannot act without God's permission.

That is one of the points of Job's sickness. When disease happened to Job, the text makes it plain that "Satan . . . afflicted Job with sores" (Job 2:7). His wife urged him to curse God. But Job said, "Shall we indeed accept good from God and not accept adversity" (Job 2:10). And again the author of the book commends Job by saying, "In all this, Job did not sin with his lips." In other words: this is a right view of God's sovereignty over Satan. Satan is real and may have a hand in our calamities, but not the final hand, and not the decisive hand. James makes clear that God had a good purpose in all Job's afflictions: "You have heard of the steadfastness of Job, and you have seen the purpose (telos) of the Lord, how the Lord is compassionate and merciful" (James 5:11). So Satan may have been involved, but the ultimate purpose was God's and it was "compassionate and merciful."

This is the same lesson we learn from 2 Corinthians 12:7 where Paul says that his thorn in the flesh was a messenger of Satan, and yet was given for the purpose of his own holiness. "To keep me from exalting myself, there was given me a thorn in the flesh, a messenger of Satan to torment me – to keep me from exalting myself!" Now, humility is not Satan's purpose in this affliction. Therefore the purpose is God's, which means that Satan here is being used by God to accomplish His good purposes in Paul's life.

There is no reason to believe that Satan is ever out of God's ultimate control. Mark 1:27 says of Jesus, "He commands even the unclean spirits, and they obey Him." And Luke 4:36 says, "With authority and power He commands the unclean spirits and they come out." In other words, no matter how real and terrible Satan and his demons are in this world, they remain subordinate to the ultimate will of God.

Natural disasters

Another kind of calamity that threatens life and health is violent weather and conditions of the earth, like earthquakes and floods and monsoons and hurricanes and tornadoes and droughts. These calamities kill hundreds of thousands of people. The testimony of the Scriptures is that God controls the winds and the weather. "He called for a famine upon the land; He broke the whole staff of bread" (Psalm 105:16). We see this same authority in Jesus. He rebukes the threatening wind and the sea, and the disciples say; "Even the wind and the sea obey Him" (Mark 4:39, 41).

Repeatedly in the Psalms God is praised as the one who rules the wind and the lightning. "He makes the winds His messengers, flaming fire His ministers" (Psalm 104:4). "He makes lightning for the rain; [he] brings forth the wind from His treasuries" (Psalm 135:7). "He causes His wind to blow and the waters to flow . . . Fire and hail, snow and clouds; Stormy wind, fulfilling His word" (Psalm 147:18; 148:8; see 78:26). Isaac Watts was right, "There's not a plant or flower below but makes your glories known; and clouds arise and tempests blow by order from your throne." This means that all the calamities of wind and rain and flood and storm are owing to God's ultimate decree. One word from him and the wind and the seas obey.

All other kinds of calamities

Other kinds of calamities could be mentioned but perhaps we should simply hear the texts that speak in sweeping inclusiveness about God's control covering them all. For example, Isaiah 45:7 says God is the "The One forming light and creating darkness, Causing well-being and creating calamity; I am the LORD who does all these." Amos 3:6 says, "If a calamity occurs in a city, has not the LORD done it?" In Job 42:2, Job confesses, "I know that you can do all things, And that no purpose of yours can be thwarted." And Nebuchadnezzar says (in Daniel 4:35), "[God] does according to his will in the host of heaven and among the inhabitants of the earth; and none can stay his hand or say to him, 'What are you doing?'" And Paul says, in Ephesians 1:11, that God is the one "who works all things after the counsel of His will."

And if someone should raise the question of sheer chance and the kinds of things that just seem to happen with no more meaning than the role of the dice, Proverbs 16:33 answers: "The lot is cast into the lap; but its every decision is from the LORD." In other words, there is no such thing as "chance" from God's perspective. He has his purposes for every roll of the dice in Las Vegas and every seemingly absurd turn of events in the universe.

This is why Charles Spurgeon, the London pastor from 100 years ago said, I believe that every particle of dust that dances in the sunbeam does not move an atom more or less than God wishes – that every particle of spray that dashes against the steamboat has its orbit, as well as the sun in the heavens – that the chaff from the hand of the winnower is steered as the stars in their courses. The creeping of an aphid over the rosebud is as much fixed as the march of the devastating pestilence – the fall of . . . leaves from a poplar is as fully ordained as the tumbling of an avalanche.

When Spurgeon was challenged that this is nothing but fatalism and stoicism, he replied, what is fate? Fate is this – Whatever is, must be. But there is a difference between that and Providence. Providence says, whatever God ordains, must be; but the wisdom of God never ordains anything without a purpose. Everything in this world is working for some great end. Fate does not say that. . . . There is all the difference between fate and Providence that there is between a man with good eyes and a blind man.

Is God the Author of Sin?

Jonathan Edwards argues that God is, Edwards says, "the perimeter . . . of sin; and at the same time, a disposer of the state of events, in such a manner, for wise, holy and most excellent ends and purposes, that sin, if it be permitted . . . will most certainly and infallibly follow."

He uses the analogy of the way the sun brings about light and warmth by its essential nature, but brings about dark and cold by dropping below the horizon. "If the sun were the proper cause of cold and darkness," he says, "it would be the fountain of these things, as it is the fountain of light and heat: and then something might be argued from the nature of cold and darkness, to a likeness of nature in the sun." In other words, "sin is not the fruit of any positive agency or influence of the most high, but on the contrary, arises from the withholding of his action and energy, and under certain circumstances, necessarily follows on the want of his influence."

Thus in one sense God wills that what he hates come to pass, as well as what he loves. Edwards says, God may hate a thing as it is in itself, and considered simply as evil, and yet . . . it may be his will it should come to pass, considering all consequences. . . . God doesn't will sin as sin or for the sake of anything evil; though it be his pleasure so to order things, that he permitting, sin will come to pass; for the sake of the great good that by his disposal shall be the consequence. His willing to order things so that evil should come to pass, for the sake of the contrary good, is no argument that he doesn't hate evil, as evil: and if so, then it is no reason why he may not reasonably forbid evil as evil, and punish it as such.

This is a fundamental truth that helps explain some perplexing things in the Bible, namely, that God often expresses His will to be one way, and then acts to bring about another state of affairs. God opposes hatred toward His people, yet ordained that his people be hated in Egypt (Genesis 12:3; Psalm 105:25 – "He turned their hearts to hate his people."). He hardens Pharaoh's heart, but commands him to let his people go (Exodus 4:21; 5:1; 8:1). He makes plain that it is sin for David to take a military census of his people, but he ordains that he does it (2 Samuel 24:1; 24:10).

He opposes adultery, but ordains that Absalom should lie with his father's wives (Exodus 20:14; 2 Samuel 12:11). He forbids rebellion and insubordination against the king, but ordained that Jeroboam and the ten tribes should rebel against Rehoboam (Romans 13:1; 1 Samuel 15:23; 1 Kings 12:15-16). He opposes murder, but ordains the murder of his Son (Exodus 20:13; Acts 4:28). He desires all men to be saved, but effectually calls only some (1 Timothy 2:4; 1 Corinthians 1:26-30; 2 Timothy 2:26).

What this means is that we must learn that God wills things in two different senses. The Bible demands this by the way it speaks of God's will in different ways. Edwards uses the terms "will of decree" and "will of command." Edwards explains: [God's] will of decree [or sovereign will] is not his will in the same sense as his will of command [or moral will] is. Therefore, it is not difficult at all to suppose that the one may be otherwise than the other: His will in both senses is his inclination.

But when we say He wills virtue, or loves virtue or the happiness of His creature; thereby is intended that virtue or the creature's happiness, absolutely and simply considered, is agreeable to the inclination of His nature. His will of decree is his inclination to a thing not as to that thing absolutely and simply, but with reference to the universality of things. So God, though He hates a thing as it is simply, may incline to it with reference to the universality of things.

Why Does God allow Evil?

It is evident from what has been said that it is not because he delights in evil as evil. Rather he "wills that evil come to pass . . . that good may come of it." What good? And how does the existence of evil serve this good end? It is a proper and excellent thing for infinite glory to shine forth; and for the same reason, it is proper that the shining forth of God's glory should be complete; that is, that all parts of his glory should shine forth, that every beauty should be proportionally effulgent, and that the beholder may have a proper notion of God? It is not proper that one glory should be exceedingly manifested, and another not at all?

Thus, it is necessary, that God's awful majesty, his authority and dreadful greatness, justice, and holiness, should be manifested. But this could not be, unless sin and punishment had been decreed; so that the shining forth of God's glory would be very imperfect, both because these parts of divine glory would not shine forth as the others do, and also the glory of His goodness, love, and holiness would be faint without them; nay, they could scarcely shine forth at all. If it were not right that God should decree and permit and punish sin, there could be no manifestation of God's holiness in hatred of sin, or in showing any preference, in his providence, of godliness before it. There would be no manifestation of God's grace or true goodness, if there was no sin to be pardoned, no misery to be saved from. How much happiness so ever he bestowed, His goodness would not be so much prized and admired. . . .

Is God less glorious because He ordained that there be evil? No, just the opposite is true. God is more glorious for having conceived and created and governed a world like this with all its evil. The effort to absolve Him by denying His foreknowledge of sin or by denying His control of sin is fatal, and a great dishonor to His word and His wisdom.

If you would see God's glory and savor His glory and magnify His glory in this world, do not remain wavering before the sovereignty of God in the face of great evil. Take His book in your hand, plead for His Spirit of illumination and humility and trust, and settle this matter, that you might be unshakable in the day of your own calamity. My prayer is that what I have said will sharpen and deepen your God-entranced world view, and that in the day of your loss you will be like Job who, when he lost all his children, fell down and worshipped, and said, "The LORD gave and the LORD has taken away. Blessed be the name of the LORD."

Why 911?

Some question why God allowed 911 and other disasters to take place? Answer: I believe that if there were no evil, we would never see God's deliverance. Because of sin evil is present. But as a result of evil we are now able to see a side of God we would otherwise not see. It is as if God were a diamond. As a diamond is turned into the light we see various reflections that it makes. As we have evil and sin in this world we see not only the loving side of God, but we see His judgment as well as His forgiveness.

What about Babies dying?

Babies dying are a result of the sin that is in the world. I believe that babies that die do go to be with the Lord. I have no proof of this other than the fact that the Lord we serve will do good. The Bible does leave us with grey areas, and the fact of whether or not babies go to heaven without confession is one of them. But just imagine this. If we knew that all babies went to heaven, we would be less likely to pray for them if they were sick. The people of old would not stress over their babies being sacrificed because they would have the assurance of them being with the Lord. On the other hand, if we thought that perhaps they went to Hell if they did not confess we would stress when they had a cold, because if it leads to death they may never see God. So the Bible is silent in this area. But we have the confidence that God knows what He is doing.

Professor Smith compared to Rabbi Kushner

Rabbi Harold S. Kushner wrote an interesting book on the subject of "When Bad Things Happen to Good People" this book is very popular and is referred to by many since the early 1980's. Let us examine some of the material and provide insight to his claims.

Kushner wrote this book as a reaction to personal tragedy--his son Aaron had premature aging, which he died from. This provoked a crisis of faith for Kushner, who is a rabbi. He wrote this book for people "who have been hurt by life", to help them find a faith that can aid in getting through their troubles, rather than making things worse.

Why do the righteous suffer?

Our answer is that God rains on the just as well as the unjust. As stated earlier, if we never saw a cloudy sky we would never really appreciate the sun. God allows us to see a greater degree of Him. Remember, He provides enough grace for us to make it through our afflictions. (Smith)

Sometimes there is reason?

Kushner argues that there are random, circumstantial sufferings, being in the wrong place at the wrong time. Kushner attributes the orderliness of the universe to God, but holds that the ordering of the universe is not complete: Some things are just circumstantial, and there is no point in looking for a reason for them (Kushner).

However we believe that God is in control. Although we do not know His plan we know that He is not surprised by anything. Everything happens for a reason. God is in control doing the work of His divine will. (Smith)

No exceptions for nice people?

Some suffering is caused by the workings of natural law. There is no moral judgment involved--natural law is blind, and God does not interfere with it. God does not intervene to save good people from earthquake or disease, and does not send these misfortunes to punish the wicked. Kushner puts great value on the orderliness of the universe's natural law, and would not want God to routinely intervene for moral reasons (Kushner).

Again I disagree with Kushner. God is the God of the universe. He has all power and He is in control. The old Humanistic idea of the universe being some cosmic time machine is anti-biblical to say the least. (Smith)

Does God help those who stop hurting themselves?

Some suffering we cause ourselves by the way we handle our initial suffering. We blame ourselves, or we take out our anger on the people who are trying to help us, or on God (Kushner).

Yes, God can help anyone who seeks Him for deliverance from their pain. (Smith)

Given that God isn't all-powerful, what good is He? (Kushner).

He is very good, excellent in fact as well as all powerful. I thought that God made the universe and it was His to control. He made us and not we ourselves, we are His people and the sheep of His pasture (psalm 100). God is all powerful. He wishes to fulfill His plan. He is not limited by any means. Don't fool yourself Rabbi, He is still in control. (Smith)

If God didn't cause our problems and can't fix them, why pray? (Kushner)

The prayers of others can make us aware that we are not facing our problems alone. And God can give us the strength of character that we need to handle our misfortunes, if we are willing to accept it. (Rabbi Kushner).

We pray because it causes us to commune with Him. He can fix our problems although He allows us the opportunity to work on some of our issues over a period of time. Remember, He is focused on building our character. (Smith)

CHAPTER 29

ANGELS DO NOT HAVE WINGS

Genesis chapter 19 (And there were two angels to Sodom).

Do Angels have wings?

The Bible does not say that all angels have wings. But the Bible does describe the Seraphim, and Cherubim have wings. But it doesn't say that a regular angel has wings. We should be careful to interject something into Scripture that isn't there.

Seraphim's each have six wings. (Isaiah 6:2 and Rev 4:6). The word "Seraphim" means "burning ones" (Ezekiel 1:4).

Cherubim: The book of Ezekiel (10:3-22) describes them as having: a face, hands, and wings (no halos),

Another type of Angel that has wings is "Thrones". They are described as having 4 faces, four wings... and are the color of burnished brass.

Some interesting facts about angels...

- Angels eat... Read Psalms 78:25
- Angels do not die. They are spiritual beings that will forever be in existence. See: Luke 20:36
- They do not have halos either

The two men describe in Genesis Chapter 19 were men. These men had no extra ordinary features on them that would have drawn attention to them; such has "wings." Angels with wings was something developed by Greek Mythology. While the seraphim have wings, angels were never described as having wings. We say, yes; others say, no: and so the subject is fairly open for investigation. Looking at this question outside of the Bible, there is certainly nothing in the nature of things to militate against the idea of angels having wings; wings, in themselves considered, would not detract from, but rather add to, the dignity and majesty of angelic beings, so far as we are able to conceive of them. There is, therefore, no objection to angels having wings, unless the Bible itself furnishes such objection. Let us then look at its testimony on this point.

The Bible furnishes no evidence that angels have wings, but that the ideas in regard to them, so current in the religious world at the present time, have been derived instead from the imagination of artists, and the representations of picture books. Such is the position of the "Millennial Harbinger," which in a recent issue vehemently argued against the idea that angels are winged beings; and yet the very paper containing said article, bore over its editorial head, and a representation of an angel flying through the midst of heaven, as liberally endowed with wings, as is usual in such illustrations.

It may be that our impressions on this point are derived somewhat, or at any rate are rendered more deep and vivid by the pictures that we almost everywhere meet, of angels with wings. But there is a question lying back of this, namely, where did the picture books get their ideas on the subject? For it cannot be supposed that any person, however imaginative, would think of such a thing as adding wings to his representations of angels, unless he had received the impression from some source higher than his imagination merely, that they were actually in possession of such members. Movies and shows like the X-men even have a winged character named Angel. Where did these people get the impression? The answer is, from the Bible, as the following considerations will show angels are represented in the Bible as flying. But, says one, are not the clouds and other things represented as flying, when we know that there are no wings employed in the case? Yes. But between angels and clouds there is just this difference: When we speak of clouds, flying, we all understand the figure at once, and are in no danger of being misled; but when angels are spoken of as flying, we have no evidence that it is a figure, and if it is, we are in danger of receiving wrong impressions. Unless, therefore, angels have wings, such language used in reference to them is not appropriate. But that no figure is employed, when angels are spoken of as flying, may be determined from this consideration, that living, animate objects are never, in the Bible, represented as flying above the earth, through the midst of heaven, and in the air, unless this is accomplished by means of wings. So when we read of angels flying, it is good proof that they have wings.

We are now prepared to read intelligently some testimony of scripture. Isaiah speaking of angels that he saw says that they did fly. Isaiah 6:2 Daniel says, "While I was speaking in prayer, even the man Gabriel, whom I had seen in the vision at the beginning, being caused to fly swiftly, touched me about the time of the evening oblation." Daniel 4:21. John says, "I beheld, and heard an angel flying through the midst of heaven, saying with a loud voice, Woe, woe, woe, to the inhabitants of the earth." Revelation 8:13. Again he says, "And I saw another angel fly in the midst of heaven."

The symbolic representations of the angelic orders were made according to divine direction with wings. Moses, when commanded to make the ark, received instruction as follows: "And thou shalt make two cherubim of gold, of beaten work shalt thou make them in the two ends of the mercy-seat; and the cherubim shall stretch forth their wings on high, covering the mercy-seat with their wings." Exodus 25:18, 20. According to this direction the cherubim were made. Chap37:7-9. When the tabernacle gave place to the temple, in addition to the cherubim on the mercy-seat, there were to large cherubim made, of ten cubits high, and stationed, one at each end of the ark in the most holy place. "And he set the cherubim within the inner house; and they stretched forth the wings of the cherubim, so that the wing of the one touched the one wall, and the wing of the other cherub touched the other wall; and their wings touched one another in the midst of the house." It was the Cherubim with the wings not an angel.1Kings 6: 27. See also chap.8, 7, and 2Chron.3:11-13.

What were these cherubim? The word cherub, of which cherubim is the plural, is defined by Webster as follows: "In the celestial hierarchy cherubs are represented as spirits next in order to seraphs." What then were these figures which were made upon the ark and in the inner house of the temple, by Moses and Solomon? They were representatives of this order of angelic beings.

The Bible expressly declares that Seraphim, which are a higher order of Angel and Cherubim have wings. Hear Isaiah's testimony: "In the year that king Uzziah died I saw also the Lord sitting upon a throne, high and lifted up, and his train filled the temple. Above it stood the seraphim: each one had six wings; with twain he covered his face, and with twain he covered his feet, and with twain he did fly." Isaiah 6:2. John, in his gospel, chapter 12:40, refers to this language of Isaiah, and says that he spoke it while he had a view of the glory of Christ. We may be sure that Isaiah saw nothing here that was not, or will not be, true in fact. He says of the seraphim plainly and positively that they each had six wings. Seraphim, according to Webster, are angels of the highest order; and if angels of the highest order have wings, there is nothing inconsistent in the idea that lower orders may also have them; this being the case with the next lower order, or cherubim, as we have already seen.

The prophet Ezekiel, also, in his sublime vision by the river of Chebar, bears testimony concerning the wings of the angelic beings. See his language in chapter 6, 9, 24; iii, 13; x, 5, 16-21. In view of this testimony of the Scriptures, we marvel greatly how any one can affirm that the Bible gives us no evidence that angels have wings. And would it not be well for those who do thus affirm, to remain a while longer under the rudimentary teaching of the primer and "picture books," before essaying to advance to the higher branches?

The Scripture is clear that angels do not have wings. The higher species do, but they do not. This comes from Greek Mythology and the Humanist viewpoint of what they thought heaven and its host looked like.

CHAPTER 30

LIKE A FLOOD GOD LIFTS UP A STANDARD

When the enemy comes in, like a flood. . .Isaiah 59:19.

Tidal Wave of the Power of God

The prophet Isaiah said it this way. "When the enemy shall come in, like a flood the Spirit of the Lord will lift up a standard against him" (Isaiah 59:19). The KJV has the comma after the word "flood" as if the enemy is the flood. However, other translations have the punctuation differently. "When the enemy comes in, like a flood the Spirit of the Lord will lift up a standard against him. "When Satan comes against the believer, the Holy Spirit comes like a flood...like a tidal wave of the power of God to drive him out. When the enemy tries to make inroads into your life, the Holy Spirit floods you with the grace and strength of God right on time. I believe Isaiah was observing from experience how the Spirit of God would drive out the enemy time and time again. If you will look back over your life, you can see the faithfulness of God to send a tidal wave of glory to turn things around in your life again and again. The devil doesn't always get his way.

"The Lord is good, a strong hold in the day of trouble, and he knoweth them that trust in him. But with an overrunning flood he will make an utter end of the place thereof, and darkness shall pursue his enemies. What do ye imagine against the Lord? He will make an utter end: affliction shall not rise up the second time" (Nahum 1:7-9)

This is a flood of the power of God that comes like a "flood" and completely destroys the enemy. God says here that He will do it so well that the affliction or oppression of the enemy will not rise up again. That is what Jesus did in His death, burial, and resurrection. Once and for all time, Satan has been defeated. Trina was healed of the brain tumor. It disappeared and has never returned...and never will. Thank God for the intercession of Jesus and the tidal wave of the Holy Spirit.

CHAPTER 31

WE DO NOT KNOW EXACTLY WHEN THE LORD WILL RETURN. It is not for you to know the times or the seasons (ACTS 1:7).

Χρονους noun

Accusative/plural/masculine

chronos khron'-os: a space of time or interval; by extension, an individual opportunity; by implication, delay -- + years old, season, space, (often-) time (-s), (a) while.

Καιρους noun

Accusative/plural/masculine
kairos kahee-ros': an occasion, i.e. set or proper time -- always, opportunity, (convenient, due) season, (due, short, while) time, a while.

How can we accurately interpret the Scriptures if we don't know anything about them? The Bible is a collection of 66 ancient Jewish scrolls written by over forty men during a two thousand year process. It is composed of many different kinds of genre of literature. There is historical narrative, poetry, hymns, theological discourse, and prophetic passages that talk about the near and distant future of men and nations and even about the End of the world.

In order for us to understand the Bible we need to have some degree of Hermeneutics, so that we may look at a particular Scripture. Each passage must be interpreted in light of its own layers of context:

1) Examine a passage in terms of its grammar, syntax, and vocabulary.
2) See a verse in the context of the paragraph.
3) Understand why that passage is in that particular place in the Bible.
4) Discover the historical, cultural, political and religious context of the author and the people to whom he is writing.

Acts 1:6, Jesus is answering His disciples, "Lord, wilt thou at this time restore again the kingdom to Israel?" Jesus then replies. 'it is not for you to know." Actually in the Koine Greek, the NOT leads out in the passage. The correct reading would be, NOT for you to know the times or the seasons. The word for times and seasons deal specifically with the correct chronology of the Lord's return and how the sequences of events will pan out.

A deep study of this passage and the Book of Revelation would be better understood after studying the book of Daniel, Ezekiel, and Apocalyptic literature. The literature gives us an idea of what was meant by what was said in this era. It is not on the same level of Scripture but it helps us to understand the time in which the people spoke and followed some obvious customs, which for us would explain why they would use certain words and phrases that they did.

For example, when Jesus describes hell He uses the term Gehenna 'Where the worm does not die and the fire is not quenched."(Mark 9:48). Here He is using a rabbinic figure of speech which was well known among the people at that time. The rabbinic literature before and during the life of Christ used the mental picture of the worms and fire connected with the city dump in the valley of Gehenna to illustrate the doctrine of everlasting punishment. Christ was not teaching that hell will involve literal worms and gnawing at literal bodies. But to look at this passage without any knowledge of literal, figurative, metaphorical language, one could easily assume that this is what will be expected in hell.

Top of Form

America has gone prophecy mad. If you read popular magazines like Time or Newsweek or if you read the technical scientific journals of our day, you will find prophetic studies on what the world will be like in the 21st Century and beyond. The secularists do not call these projections concerning the future "prophecy" for that word has too much of a religious connotation. Instead of "prophecy" they use the word SCENARIO, which means to outline the coming events. I am sure that you have been required to read much in the area of secular scenarios. Some of you have read 1984, The Biological Time Bomb, or any number of the multitude of books which seek to tell us what the future holds.

The Christian in the 20th Century can take advantage of the present popularity of prophetic studies in the secular world by putting forth intelligibly the divine, inspired scenario of coming events. While the world can only guess about the future, the Christian has a sure word of prophecy (II Pet. 1:19). We know through Scripture the main points of the future. We must, therefore, be prepared to give a logical and reasonable reply to anyone who questions us concerning the prophetic hope within our hearts. This will be in obedience to I Pet. 3:15, 16.

- We should be prepared to answer the secular world when it asks us concerning the Christian scenario. How?
- Make Christ the Lord of our life. Without the new birth, you will not be personally prepared to experience the future.
- Have a prepared answer: a knowledgeable and intelligent understanding of Biblical prophecy.

  Manifest a proper attitude toward others
  meekness: humility
  fear: respect

There are some essential Christian view points that are widely held by most Prophecy Teachers:

1) Christ is coming back to this earth literally, visibly, and personally.
2) Eventually all the dead bodies of all departed souls will be resurrected.
3) The Christians alive at the Second Coming will be translated without tasting death.
4) All the Non-Christians will stand before Christ on the Day of Judgment.
5) All Christians will one day stand before Christ for Judgment.
6) This present world will be destroyed by fire and a new earth and new heavens will be created.
7) The righteous will go into eternal conscious blessedness and the wicked into eternal conscious torment.

Christ is sitting on His throne and reigning right now over His kingdom. We don't look forward to the reign of Christ in the future because we are experiencing that reign in the present.

1. Luke. 1:31-33
2. Ephesians. 1:20-22.
3. Revelation. 1:5.

The present church age is the Kingdom of Christ.

1. Colossians. 1:13.
2. 1 Corinthians. 15:23-28.
3. Matthew 13:41.

When Christ returns there will be a general resurrection of all the dead.

1. John 5:25-29.
2. John 11:24.
3. 1 Corinthians. 15-22.

When Christ returns, it means the Day of Judgment and the end of the world.

1. Matthew 24:3.
2. I Corinthians. 15:23, 24.
3. II Peter. 3:12-14.
4. Matthew 25: 31-46.

The common denominator: No Christian can rightfully set a date for Christ's return for no one knows the exact hour or day of His return. (Matt. 24:36, 42, 44; 25:13). The imminent return theory, according to Dispensationalist, Christ's return is possible this very second. It is always at hand, ready to happen at any moment. There are no signs or prophecies that must precede Christ's coming for the church. It will be an absolute surprise to the Christian for it will come "as a thief in the night." This means Christ's return will be sudden, without warning, a surprise, and a secret. According to this theory, Christ's return was imminent for the apostles for they looked for

Christ's return to happen suddenly and without warning. It has always been imminent through the ages.

The following pages point out the Scriptural evidence which supports the doctrine that Christ will return at the end of the world to gather his people, judge the wicked, and usher in the eternal state.

I Corinthians. 15:51-54 compared with Isaiah 25: 6-8

In verse 54, Paul says the prophecy of Isaiah 25:8 will be fulfilled at the time of the resurrection and translation of the church. (vs. 51-53).

Isaiah 25:8 states the swallowing up of death will take place at the end of the tribulation (chapter. 24: 20-25:5), in connection with the setting up of the everlasting kingdom (chapter. 25: 6-9).

In I Corinthians. 15: 51-54, the resurrection and translation of the church will take place at the end of the tribulation in connection with the setting up of the everlasting kingdom,

Christ will stay in heaven until "the time of the restoration of all things." This refers to the judgment of the world. He will not return until He comes to restore all things under His authority. This can only mean He cannot return until the tribulation is over.

All the Greek terms employed in the New Testament to describe the coming of Christ refer to a visible glorious coming. These various terms are used interchangeably. The only coming of Christ found in the Greek New Testament is the glorious post-tribulation return of Christ.

Second Coming of Christ

Who knows when Christ will return? Prediction books have even been written picking the exact day of Jesus' return. These books may sell many copies, but they mislead their readers. There's one guarantee: As soon as someone predicts the day or time of Jesus Christ's second coming, that prediction is wrong. Why? Simply, only God the Father knows when it will be -- Jesus doesn't even know. Jesus told His disciples:

"No one knows about that day or hour, not even the angels in heaven, nor the Son, but only the Father." "Two men will be in the field; one will be taken and the other left. Two women will be grinding with the hand mill; one will be taken and the other left." "Therefore keep watch, because you do not know on what day your Lord will come." (Matthew 24:36, 40 & 42)

Second Coming of Christ - Signs for Keeping Watch We could just shrug our shoulders and casually wait for the Second Coming of Christ. However, Jesus wants us to "keep watch." A great way to keep watch is to know what the Bible reveals about upcoming events and compare those to what we see happening today. There are nearly 100 biblical passages discussing the Second Coming of Jesus Christ.

Conclusion

No one should be dogmatic on such issues as Bible prophecy. Good and godly men have disagreed down through the centuries. The views above are not final, but are our own feeble attempts to think through the issues and passages that apply to this doctrine. We have a general idea when Jesus will return, and how He will return, but we cannot be overly aggressive with our opinions.

Suggested Reading

When is it Right to Fight, by Robert A. Morey. Bethany House Publishers

How Should We Then Live? Francis A. Schaeffer. Crossway Books

Encyclopedia of Bible Difficulties, by Gleason L. Archer. Zondervan.

Scientific America, February 1960, page 132.

The Qur'an Translation. Tahrike Tarsile Qur'an, Inc

God Sovereign and Man Free. N.L. Rice. Spinkle Publications

The Islamic Invasion, Dr. Bob Morey. Harvest House Publishers

The Defense of the Faith, Cornelius Van Til. Presbyterian and Reformed publishing company.

Encyclopedia Britannica, 1958, Volume 7, page 766.

Don't Die Before You Live. Dr. Allen Smith. Papito Publishing.

The Ten Commandments. Dr. L. Schlesinger and Rabbi Vogel. Harper Collins publishing

Hermeneutics. Henry Virkler. Baker Book House

The Road Less Traveled. M. Scott Peck. Touchstone book.

What is a Man? Waller R Newell, Regan books

Made in the USA
San Bernardino, CA
15 July 2018